THE
HOLISTIC
DIVORCE

THE HOLISTIC DIVORCE

A Practical 10-Step Process *for* Healing

OLGA NADAL

Pono Maui PUBLISHING

THE HOLISTIC DIVORCE
A Practical 10-Step Process for Healing

ISBN 978-1-5445-2454-2 Hardcover
978-1-5445-2453-5 Paperback
978-1-5445-2452-8 Ebook

I dedicate this book to Ian, mi amorzote and one of my greatest teachers, who entered my heart disguised as a "nerdy geek with a tie."

To Carmen and Alex, my children and the reason behind my mission to change the paradigm of divorce once and for all.

And Marie Forleo, who inspired me to start this movement by asking me to "go out there and make waves." This book is the first one...

CONTENTS

ACKNOWLEDGMENTS

I have worn many hats in my life, from entrepreneur, to mother, wife, and student of many disciplines, but nothing I have experienced compares to becoming an author. It is one thing to write a book; it is another to journey inward to bring forth all your gifts and vulnerabilities and pour them into a permanent format for the world to see. It is my hope this book will change people's lives and turn the concept of divorce from one riddled with trauma to an opportunity for growth.

I truly could not have done it without the support and guidance of many wonderful souls. I want to acknowledge all my coaching clients who authorized me to share their divorce stories and all those who allowed me to guide them through their transitions. Without their faith in me and my system, I could not have perfected the methodology I describe in this book and teach to my students at The Holistic Divorce Institute.

My husband deserves most of the credit for this book coming to fruition. He supported me on all levels and kept pushing me gently to bring this project to the forefront of my long list of commitments. He graciously provided me the space, time, and resources to focus solely on writing while I drastically reduced the number of one-on-one clients I coached.

I would also like to thank the team at Scribe Media that helped me stay on track with all the deadlines and handled most of the technical complexities that I could not even begin to comprehend.

And finally, I would like to acknowledge all the teachers and spiritual guides that this beautiful Hawaiian land I call home has brought to me. Maui has been the sacred sanctuary that taught me everything I know about healing and the spirit of Aloha that I hope this book will spread all over the world.

ABOUT THE AUTHOR

Olga Nadal is the founder of Divorce for Love and CEO of The Holistic Divorce Institute. Despite feeling lost and grief-ridden during her own divorce process, she managed to achieve an enviable low-conflict divorce—one that allowed her to thrive in the next chapter of her life.

Wanting to save others the pain she went through, Olga used her experience to create the divorce coaching methodology that has helped her many clients achieve the same level of success. Now, she shares that process in *The Holistic Divorce*, expanding her mission to take the chaos and loneliness out of divorce and transform it into a catalyst for personal growth.

Connect with her online at www.olganadal.com or on Instagram @divorceforlove.

INTRODUCTION

⌒

Last time I checked, seven out of the ten books at the top of the nonfiction bestseller list were on the subject of relationships. Topics ranged from finding your soulmate and getting them to commit, to surviving the rough patches and fixing the unfixable. Yet not a single one of the relationship gurus and their books spoke to our most neglected need for education on how to end marriages in a civilized and holistic manner. My work and passion revolve around this one objective, and this book is the synthesis of the methodology I created based on my own divorce and the combined experiences of my clients as they applied it to their own transitions.

I like to say that relationships are separate entities from the individuals involved and have their own life cycles and expiration dates. For some, that date comes when they leave this world. For others, that date correlates with a variety of factors: they grew apart, became resentful, got bored, evolved at different speeds, wanted different things, could not agree on anything, betrayed trust, damaged loyalty, changed interests, had irreconcilable differences, or my favorite explanation to why a relationship ends, life happened. Whatever the reason, we need to start acknowledging that many—I would dare to say the majority—of us are not designed to remain in a marriage forever, especially the first one into which we enter.

We have to make peace with the reality that a bond that is outgrown, or in many cases, that has become far from beneficial, can be severed without creating a soul-shattering and traumatizing event. If you learn how to make the transition while minimizing the impact, the experience can be a catalyst for tremendous growth, emotional intelligence, and better alignment with your true self, meaning the self in the present moment, not the one who married years ago without fully knowing themselves or what they wanted from life. This is perfectly OK, and this book will show you how it is acceptable to want more and to not settle for good, but to instead seek extraordinary love.

Divorce has been villainized since its inception as the root cause for the disintegration of the family structure. I believe divorce is the remedy needed to stop a harmful bond from hurting the members of that family. The questionable belief that humans are supposed to form a long-lasting union with someone they chose at one time of their evolution—a union that can only be dissolved by death—has proven unsustainable for a high number of couples. For centuries, those who found themselves in loveless, or worse, abusive marriages had no recourse but to accept their fates and resign themselves to staying in damaging partnerships. We are fortunate to have the option to both legally and morally remove ourselves from the marriage and have a chance at a more fulfilled future, with or without a partner.

I have often said I am not pro-divorce nor pro-marriage, just pro happy people. Society perpetuates a damaging glorification of staying married at all costs, even to the detriment of the mental health of both the individual and their children. The fundamental takeaway, as we will explore, is that you have permission to do what is best for you, and what will inevitably benefit your children, and even your ex. This is not an exaggeration or metaphor. I have had many clients tell me that with time, their disgruntled spouses who were radically opposed to divorce have thanked them for taking the brave step they could not take themselves.

The biggest issues those considering divorce face are a lack of information tailored to their specific needs, a complete disregard for acknowledging the overriding influence emotions can play, and negative messaging about the process and aftermath that society has quietly accepted without questioning. It has been my mission to change every single one of these obstacles to clear the path for those who, in my opinion, are courageous and honest enough to admit when it is time to end a cycle. I have tirelessly researched ways to bridge the gap between what people presume divorce is and what it can be once you accept responsibility for your part in the unfolding. My clients were able to make decisions that they did not second-guess or regret later, thanks to becoming emotionally sober through our coaching before engaging in the legal process.

Divorce sometimes resembles getting blackout drunk, being handed the keys to your car, and being told to get yourself home. We either get in the car and have hope as our only strategy to make it there safe, or we hand the keys to someone else (usually a lawyer, friend, or relative) and trust them completely. My approach is different: as a Holistic Divorce Coach, I will sit with you by the side of the road while you purge everything that is toxic and help you sip water until you sober up. Once the poison has left your body, you can choose either yourself or someone else to drive home, knowing you will not get lost or taken advantage of on your way there. Divorce can be a treacherous transition or a beautiful rite of passage that teaches you lessons that will serve you for the rest of your life. You get to choose which path you take.

The core of the methodology I created around the Holistic Divorce proves that the advance of new approaches reducing conflict and need for litigation are the basis for a passage that completely transforms you into a better version of yourself. Gone are the days when divorce will invariably destroy your financial, emotional, and even social standing. The managing of emotions and the skills you can learn, if you choose to have a Holistic Divorce, contain the seeds for healing not just your current relationship but even previous traumas caused by interpersonal arrangements that you did not understand.

In this book, you will take an intimate look at the emotions driving your decision to stay or go: shame, guilt, grief, anger, and fear. I will provide you with the clues to understand the messages hidden behind those feelings so you can decipher what you have had all along: the answers to all your questions. Should I stay or go? Will I be financially secure? Will the kids be OK or traumatized? Will I find love again? In short, you will reconnect with your intuition and the well of wisdom inside of you that knows which decisions are right for YOU.

I also dive deep into the divorce journey and all the stages you must go through—or as I prefer to say, grow through—to ultimately make peace with your final decision. It is a dark road ahead if we don't know what to expect, but if we are prepared for each step along the way, we will find the peace and clarity we seek. Although each divorce is a world of its own, there are many similarities that are universal and help us feel understood when we realize we are not alone or going crazy. If you were to climb Mount Everest, would you do it based on the advice of someone who opted to forgo researching the terrain or using a professional guide, and who inevitably did not make it to the top? Or would you rely on someone who took all the necessary steps and was therefore successful on their climb? If you want to turn the divorce experience from traumatizing to empowering, using the principles of Holistic Divorce and the expertise of a Holistic Divorce Coach is essential.

We used to be ashamed of wanting to leave, but now we are shamed for staying out of fear. I believe it is a step in the right direction to no longer receive recognition for staying in an unhappy marriage just for the sake of the children or because "it is not so bad." Wanting great, not just good, refusing to settle, and aiming higher are, in my opinion, all the reasons needed to pursue a future that truly aligns with you. When we remove the classic excuses to leave—the children will be traumatized, I will never find love again, I'm too (fill in the blank) to pull this off—all that is left are the emotions of divorce blocking our exit. Understanding those emotions and how to manage them so they do not spin the process out of control is what I have dedicated my work to.

As much as I integrate the logistical and the emotional components through my Holistic Divorce methodology, I dedicate most of this book to understanding the depth of those emotions and outlining the ten-step process I created for healing the divorce wounds. The legalities of each situation are pretty straightforward once you remove the emotional drivers. For example, no matter how upset you are about your spouse's infidelity, you have to know that child support and alimony payments will be determined according to established calculations that do not factor in your ideas of right and wrong. It's better to handle those valid emotions in a setting outside of the legal system. Guidelines also differ from state to state and must be directly correlated to your particular arrangements analyzed on a one-on-one basis by your divorce coach and lawyer. Most of my clients end up saving thousands of dollars in legal fees because they only contact their attorney to handle the legal matters of the process instead of using them as a therapist, coach, or friend onto whom they unload their emotional burdens.

Most of my clients are female, and I assume most of my readers are as well. As you will learn in these pages, women are leading the change around divorce, and I do not think it is by coincidence. We are truly rising from systems that kept women oppressed for centuries, and being chained to a man we do not love anymore is no longer acceptable. I honor all those women who are paving the way to end their marriages without a trail of destruction left behind, and it is my hope this book will guide them toward that goal.

I also want to give credit to the men who are rising to the occasion, and if you are a male reading these pages, I applaud your desire to revert the paradigm of confrontation divorce used to be. I have worked with some remarkable men who fully embodied the principles of the Holistic Divorce and are setting a great example for future generations. It is my ultimate wish that my words will inspire both men and women to cooperate instead of annihilate each other as they complete their marriage cycle and move to their next great chapter.

1

THE CRISIS THAT SHOWED US HOW FINISHED OUR MARRIAGES REALLY WERE

I first heard the news about lockdowns to curb the spread of coronavirus from a client who lives in north Italy. She had finally worked up the courage and confronted the million emotions to conclude that her marriage had ended. She signed the lease for her beautiful new apartment and had everything lined up to start her new life, yet she was now on our Zoom call wondering aloud if she would be able to move while the stay-at-home orders were in place. She was riddled with anxiety as all her hard work seemed to evaporate in an instant, and she could not fathom the possibility of living with her spouse again.

Since the beginning of the pandemic, divorce and relationship breakups have been on the rise, and there seems to be no chance of reversing this trend anytime soon. When governments around the world followed suit and asked citizens to stay at home for an indefinite amount of time, my heart dropped. I thought about my many clients who would have a hard time being stuck at home with spouses who were only communicating with them through lawyers or mediators. My soul ached for children whose safe space from the hostile environment at home was school. I also had an emotional time sharing the utter terror of those who were in situations of domestic abuse and might now have to share their space with their aggressor 24/7.

We cannot deny that the lockdowns forced many couples to take a close look at their relationships. Many marriages were surviving on the premise of living almost completely independent lives from their spouses. Their parenting had become a game of tag, and their intimate moments were a thing of the past. If they were still civilized and somewhat cordial, the overexposure that the stay-at-home order brought might have been the tipping point in realizing they were not meant to be together anymore.

Those with marriages already strained and on the brink of extinction stood no chance to make it to the other side unscathed. Yet almost no one would be ready for this unexpected catalyst of their divorce. If I have seen one common denominator in all nasty divorces, it is that one of the parties was unprepared for what was ahead. That is why I began to create resources for the avalanche of people who would be needing my services in the near future: those opting for divorce after being confronted with the reality that the more time they spent together, the less in love they were.

The best way to ensure a drama-free divorce is to prepare for it. When it comes to divorce, leaving anything to chance is a sure ticket to the wildest ride of your life.

I have a prediction that makes some feel very uneasy: the divorce rate will, within this decade, rise beyond the current 50 percent to somewhere above 80 percent. This might sound like an alarming statistic, but I do not believe this should be a concern or confirmation that our social fabric is disintegrating. As our society is undertaking major changes in the ways we relate, work, and communicate, all while lifespans grow longer, we are simply adjusting to a completely new reality. We live longer and have more financial independence. Women enjoy more freedoms. A collective awakening is resulting in entire generations adapting to these shifts. The sooner we accept the new reality that most relationships will NOT last forever, the sooner we can work toward solving the real problem.

The tragedy is not that most marriages will end in divorce; the real problem is *how* we divorce. Ignorance, unprocessed emotions, and lack of conflict management and communication skills are the real issues. They materialize in the form of time-consuming and astronomically expensive legal battles that leave all parties in a disadvantageous position. The current average divorce is finalized in just over a year and costs from thousands of dollars to over six figures in legal and court fees. The majority of these cases end with a settlement that does not fully satisfy the parties and an extremely damaged relationship. This makes co-parenting and moving on truly challenging.

It is my mission to shift the current paradigm from one that portrays divorce as a horrible, traumatic event to be avoided at all costs to one that shows it as a catalyst for profound growth and as the necessary step toward closing a chapter so you can move on to the next step of your evolution. I completely disagree with the politically incorrect view of stigmatizing divorce and the omnipresent criticism of those who choose this path. It is my dream that we will soon live in a world where transitioning from marriage to divorce is a passage full of support and understanding, without emotional distress and societal exile.

If you are about to embark on the journey of divorce, it is my utmost desire that you find in my work the hope, inspiration, and resources to achieve the wonderful transformation from miserably married to happily divorced. I share in this book everything I have learned as a divorce coach and have distilled into my methodology: The 10-Step Program for a Holistic Divorce. You will also find the inspiring stories of those brave souls who decided to change their divorce story and the trajectory of their lives by working with the skills and tools I taught them. I showcase examples from my own clients (names have been changed to protect their identity) to help familiarize you with the methodology I created. That being said, I know of many other wonderful divorce coaches who can assist you. If my approach does not resonate, please find other mentors and teachers to assist you in having a divorce of which you can be proud.

My purpose when coaching clients one-on-one is to teach them that the impossible divorce is possible. Emotions and logistics can be handled in a holistic manner to avoid animosity and trauma— you just have to learn how. With each client I help navigate toward a low-conflict resolution, we show society how we can remove conflict, anger, resentment, and the spiraling of other negative emotions from the process of divorce. I hope you also choose this path and get to the other side of divorce more whole and fulfilled. But first, I'd like to share my own divorce journey.

One Marriage, Three Divorces

I call my story "One Marriage, Three Divorces." It is the recollection of the ending of my own marriage, the ending of my parents' marriage, and my dad's second divorce.

I got married on a beach on Maui in 2003 to a wonderful man with whom I would move from Spain to a little island in Hawaii. For someone who had repeatedly announced that I would never, ever tie the knot, this was a huge turnaround.

Why was I adamantly against marriage? My parents' (far from pleasant) marriage and the inevitable nasty divorce they tried to avoid for over a decade. I am the poster child for how much damage unhappy marriages can create. Watching my parents' marriage erode until love was replaced with anger and resentment left a profound mark. The divorce, as bad as it was, finally signaled the end of the hostile war zone we lived in for so many years. My siblings and I felt many emotions, but the most prevalent was *relief*.

My parents' divorce followed the pattern I call "Old-School Divorce." They tried to save a dysfunctional marriage at any cost until becoming completely jaded by their inability to make it work. Then, they pursued the only model that was available: litigating lawyers that created unnecessary conflict to prolong the process while promoting discord and communication breakdown between my parents.

In the Old-School Divorce, dishonorable behavior is justified, even if your moral compass is trying to ring the alarm. People feel entitled to as much as they can possibly get without any consideration for what is fair. Dealing with the emotions of divorce is not even part of the equation, which creates massive amounts of emotional wounding. There has to be a winner and a loser, which is determined by who can afford the best—usually most expensive—lawyer. The whole process is traumatizing, expensive, and exhausting. Everybody feels like they lost, and nobody is satisfied.

My parents' divorce ended up with a rather unbalanced distribution of assets. My father kept most of the financial resources and was not required to fulfill any custody arrangements. For years, we would only see him on the rare occasion that suited his schedule, and our lifestyle turned upside down as our stay-at-home mom tried to make ends meet. I survived what would surely ruin any childhood, and sadly, I would have to deal with another awful divorce, courtesy of my dad and his second wife.

Just as I was in the middle of the peaceful dissolution of my own marriage, my father passed away. He had divorced his second wife a few years prior. Yet they never reached a financial agreement, meaning my siblings and I would have to partake in a three-year, costly legal battle to settle the case with his ex. I know my father was still caught up in the Old-School Divorce mentality and thought he would replicate the same strategy. Yet his second wife would not accept being the loser in the settlement, so she turned the tables on him by getting an even more ruthless lawyer who was happy to stretch the process out. He was getting paid handsomely. So why not?

It was beyond strange being thrown into the very style of divorcing that I seek to dismantle. I joke that it was a good education and enabled me to serve my clients better. I had not been afraid of my marriage ending, but I was terrified of my relationship with my soon-to-be ex deteriorating because we had a conflict-ridden divorce.

I look back at my own divorce and see objectively where I succeeded and where I could have done better. For years, I felt very proud that my ex and I managed to do the whole process without hiring lawyers. We negotiated our marital settlement, and after some back and forth, we managed to agree on the financial and custodial arrangements. With hindsight, I can now tell you that is not the approach I recommend for most of my clients. I did consult with a family lawyer a friend recommended because I wanted to know our rights and get my expectations right. What I got instead was a rather high bill to listen to a barrage of derogatory comments intended to convince me that I was crazy for not taking an aggressive approach and demanding I keep everything. This lawyer would not accept my explanation that I did not want everything; I wanted fair, and for me, that meant 50/50. She insisted I could keep ownership of our family home, our investment property, a large stake in our businesses, and most custody, which would prompt child-support payments. Due to my visa status, I was not allowed to work outside my businesses, so she pushed that I also demand spousal support. This interaction made me feel like involving lawyers would be a huge mistake, but now I know that not all lawyers are like the one with whom I met.

I am fortunate to have worked with many wonderful, collaborative divorce lawyers while assisting my clients who had expressed the same disgust I felt in that lawyer's office. These lawyers have also corroborated my suspicion that I could have never gotten all of those demands fulfilled without a long and costly legal battle, one that would have drained our resources and still concluded without getting everything I might've asked for. Not to mention, it would have ruined the amicable relationship with my ex and caused damage to our children, who would have been deprived of spending time with their dad. I declined to retain that first lawyer's services and felt so discouraged by the whole experience that instead of trying to find a collaborative lawyer or someone more receptive to my fair approach, I decided we would not involve them at all. This was a dangerous move, and I do not recommend it unless you have no assets, liabilities, or children in common. I was fortunate we were able to reach fair agreements, but if I did not have the business and financial knowledge from my entrepreneurial background, I might have signed an agreement that would come back to haunt me.

Another of my regrets is staying in the "Limbo of Divorce" for much longer than necessary. This is the place where you are so paralyzed by fear that you take no action, staying in suffering without any resolution in sight. I remained there for three years until I hired my life coach. Although she did not specialize in divorce, the transformation I experienced in the months we worked together gave me the confidence and clarity I needed to achieve a healthy divorce. Her work had such an influence on me that I decided to become a life coach specializing in divorce coaching. I now train others in the methodology I crafted to ensure that both the emotional and logistical sides are considered equally.

The part of my own divorce experience that I do not regret is sharing custody 50/50. This is one area where we achieved a triple win-win-win victory: my ex, our kids, and I all won with this arrangement. However, I certainly did not feel like that would be the case, when at first, I was terrified of not seeing my kids every single day. I now fully appreciate the moments when we are together and I am completely engaged, and I also love the times when I know they are enjoying their dad, and I can focus on my passions and new relationship.

Although people have gasped at how many financial assets I left on the table so my ex would not have to struggle, I still feel it was the right decision. I honestly could not have had a clear conscience knowing that I took more just because the system allowed me to or because society deemed me crazy not to. I have always created my own financial abundance, and I refused to give in to the narrative that no one can ever recover from a divorce so they better get as much as possible. I am now in a much more affluent state than during my marriage, and I truly believe the universe always rewards generosity and kindness.

My deepest regret is not asking for the right help when I needed it. Presuming that because I had handled plenty of challenges in my life, I could navigate this transition on my own, and not wanting to burden friends and family, I suffered the emotional roller coaster of divorce in isolation. I was sure I could handle on my own the feelings that every ending evokes, yet I almost did not make it when these emotions overtook me completely. It is a shame that we do not share our divorce stories and honor the ending of our marriages so we can heal collectively.

I truly hope no man or woman has to face this critical life passage on their own. I hope each person is surrounded by a tribe that supports them unconditionally. I dream of a day when we celebrate the ending of a marriage as grandiosely as its inception. That might be the day we see marriage as what it is: a marvelous learning chapter out of this wonderful book we call life.

The Problem Is Not That We Divorce— It Is *How* We Divorce

I don't believe our current divorce rate (one in two marriages) is a consequence of living in a dysfunctional society. I've seen firsthand the cathartic effect divorce has on many people. It makes me believe that although the process is difficult, there is plenty of magic on the other side. Let me be clear: this is not an attack on the institution of marriage. I believe marriage is to be respected and cherished as a solid foundation on which to create a thriving life, and currently, it's the only option offered to those who want a committed relationship. But happiness is more important than marriage. I am in favor of happy people who can in turn be happy parents and better members of society. If that means a marriage has to end, by all means, let it end.

The majority of my coaching clients have seen their lives greatly improved after they ended their unhappy marriages. The issue is not the divorce rate—the real tragedy is that we have created a narrative around divorce that involves shame, judgment, anger, bitterness, and behaviors that would be morally dubious under most circumstances but that we justify because we have collectively agreed that divorce is dirty business.

Ask anyone what first comes to mind when you say the word "divorce." Most answers revolve around conflict, expense, and emotional exhaustion. It's true divorce has been that way since it became legal, but society has changed dramatically in the last few decades, and a huge paradigm shift has occurred. We are beginning to accept that most relationships are not meant to last forever, and the ending does not have to be a bitter battle. The emphasis is not on the reasons why the marriage ended but on how to make this transition a catalyst for empowerment.

There is an ever-growing movement of amicable divorces, conscious separations, and respectful marriage endings. There are more professionals entering the field to offer support beyond the traditional litigation system. You can now hire a divorce coach who will simplify and guide you through the process. You can be assisted by a mediator to reach agreements with even the most controversial of partners. And most importantly, you can find communities of like-minded individuals that instead of guilt-tripping, will support you unconditionally.

Let me be clear: there is a tremendous amount of anxiety when ending a relationship, and adding children and assets to that scenario stirs the internal turmoil to a degree that few people are willing to face. However, I want to stress that it is possible to end it without animosity and that we all have the courage and strength to do so; you might just have to find help to guide you. Our fathers and mothers certainly did not have these options. That's why a conflict-ridden and emotionally devastating system was established. But we do have a choice:

> *To perpetuate the myth that your divorce will be one of the most traumatic experiences of your life, OR to ensure that you have a divorce of which you can be proud.*

I challenge the myth that the goal of a marriage or a committed long-term relationship is to remain together forever even if the individuals' needs and desires are being suppressed to maintain the bond. I am a living and breathing example that the impossible divorce is possible. I am proof that you can have an uncomplicated divorce and a civilized relationship with your ex, that your children will be perfectly normal, and that you will get another chance to find a loving partner. My clients corroborate that they, too, made the impossible divorce possible.

Deb's Divorce Story

I wish you could meet Deb. She is the reason why many of us believe in romance, fairy-tale weddings, and the bliss of motherhood. She can also add "successful divorce" to her long list of achievements.

Deb married a man, let's call him Ken, who was the most coveted bachelor in their South Carolina town. They were the perfect couple and seemed to redefine the concept of marriage as a wonderland where you become happier and more beautiful with every passing anniversary. Even after giving birth to three kids and adopting a fourth, Deb was the poster child for all things motherhood and housewife bliss. She seemed to enjoy every minute of it—except when the seemingly innocent day-drinking turned into afternoon fun and eventually, a recurring nighttime horror show.

Ken showed no sympathy for the woman he claimed to love so dearly but whose untreated depression and anxiety was quickly eroding their beautifully constructed facade of pleasantries and joy. He threatened to divorce her and take the kids if she did not stop drinking right away. She tried and failed to do it on her own, then begged Ken for a second chance at a rehab center. Now you would think that Ken would lean into his promise of loving Deb in sickness and in health and would agree to her request for help. Sadly, he was more preoccupied with what people would think. He demanded she sober up at home, while taking care of the kids, keeping the house spotless, and satisfying him sexually, or else.

She begged one more time and asked to at least see a therapist to help her deal with the unbelievable emotional pain that made her drink until passing out. He said as long as it was done privately, he was OK with it. But he wanted to see results right away. Deb began searching for therapists online who could help her with her alcohol addiction. She came across one of my posts where I talked about how going sober for two years was crucial to going through the challenges of divorce. She was curious and began reading to the point where four hours had passed, and she was sobbing through all my Instagram posts and blogs. She decided to quit drinking, but not to keep a man who showed such little empathy and compassion. She would do it for herself and her children so she could divorce Ken and marry a man who truly understood and loved her.

When we had our first consultation, I was reluctant to take her on as a client. I wanted to help her have a divorce she could be proud of, but knowing firsthand how immensely difficult it is to kick alcoholism, I was not sure she could do that and divorce at the same time. I asked her to work with a therapist first, then once her drinking was under control, we would tackle her divorce—which, by the way, she had not told Ken about it. She insisted the two went hand in hand, and that she would stop drinking as long as she was making progress toward getting a divorce. I understood, and my intuition told me not to abandon someone who was determined to get better and seeking support.

I am happy to report that Deb did stop drinking. For those who are curious or skeptical, she was able to do it with the help of ceremonies involving plant medicine in the jungle of Costa Rica (you can find more about this in my next book *Rice and Beans: The Journey Back to My Heart*). Following my ten-step program, Deb became a Jedi of emotional mastery, managing to clearly and calmly let Ken know they were getting a divorce. With my guidance, she practiced how to have meaningful conversations with him, their children, their families, and their relatives without encountering resistance. I introduced her to a collaborative lawyer and a financial advisor, experts in quick and inexpensive divorces. Deb and her husband signed final agreements just eight months after she started working with me, and to this day, they maintain a civilized relationship and are fantastic co-parents.

The Old-School Divorce

Once upon a time, you *had* to remain married until you died because the option of divorce simply did not exist. In 1857, the first divorce law in England came into effect, and America caught up pretty quickly, with divorce rates increasing rapidly. What began as a process only affordable to the upper class became commonplace in the twenty-first century. Access to lawyers is now easy, and thanks to our online culture, you don't even need a lawyer. You can fork out a few hundred dollars to complete the whole process and never see the inside of a courtroom.

Thank goodness twentieth-century law did away with the "fault" requirement! Previously, you had to prove your spouse had committed adultery, was mentally unstable, or was extremely abusive/cruel. Today, you do not need to justify your decision to divorce. It can even be a unilateral decision, meaning your spouse does not have to consent to it. Other factors that have brought the divorce rate to over 50 percent are the increasing financial independence of women and divorce being the most accepted approach by society.

Currently, the median marriage length in America hovers around eleven years, and the majority of divorces (more than 70 percent) are filed by women. Contrary to popular belief, 90 percent of these divorces settle out of court. I want to stress this unknown fact because most people believe their divorce will inevitably end up in court, and they use that idea to justify lawyering up as soon as the word "divorce" is uttered. This mistaken logic continues with the belief that the more expensive the retainer, the better the lawyer and your chances of getting everything you want, revenge included. Sadly, this misconception could not be further from the truth and can be a costly mistake.

The main reasons why people find themselves in court are because their expectations were not efficiently managed and/or they were improperly guided by the hired professionals. One of the first steps I take when working with clients is to ensure that we manage their expectations, so they do not end up bitter and broke. Mismanaged expectations arise when you believe you are entitled to more than you legally are and when the cost to get what is legally yours is higher than the value of those things. In both cases, reconsidering expectations works in your favor.

I know what you are thinking: *if the law says it's mine, then I will fight tooth and nail to get it.* This approach could cost you dearly. Your spouse's lawyers might be incredibly crafty at interpreting the law in a way that bogs down any progress and drains your savings in the process. Even if you are disputing over something that legally belongs to you, I suggest carefully analyzing if the cost/value ratio is worth it, so you are not forced to give it up after burning through your financial resources.

Parties who fail to negotiate terms on their own or with the help of their lawyers and/or mediators will likely also end up with a judge making all the final decisions. Although there is a place and time when the courtroom is needed, for the majority of cases, this is the worst direction a divorce can take. It is the ultimate loss of control on the final settlements. Generally, none of the parties get what they want, and many experience no sense of justice or fairness with the resolution the judge delivers.

Another sad reality is that many divorces are completely hijacked by the professionals hired to help. This is particularly the case with lawyers who escalate conflict instead of reducing it, overestimate expectations, and fail to bring other experts such as divorce financial analysts and divorce coaches, if needed, to deal with areas they do not fully comprehend. The good news is that this type of divorce and its devastating effects is becoming less prevalent. People are now opting for more civilized and amicable solutions that are less expensive and emotionally damaging. Along these lines, I would like to introduce you to what I call the Holistic Divorce. It is based on my own story and most of my clients' stories. It might sound too good to be true at first, but stay with me, and I'll show you how it may be possible for you too. But first: a cautionary tale. Rosie's story is, unfortunately, a reminder of how costly the Old-School Divorce can be.

Rosie's Divorce Story

Rosie's Instagram message to me was one of the main reasons I created the Holistic Divorce Institute, with a mission to train an army of divorce coaches whose purpose is to guide and protect people just like her. My heart broke reading about the story of destruction and misery that her divorce caused her and her family. Because of it, Rosie had entered a deep depression and could not continue to operate her thriving business. The most sickening part was that as we exchanged messages back and forth, it became more apparent she was in a war zone created by a pair of unscrupulous lawyers who fed on her naivete and inability to handle the emotions of divorce.

Rosie's situation very much reminded me of the movie *Marriage Story*, the 2019 Netflix film about a couple who decide they want to separate amicably, but as the lawyers begin playing their dirty tricks, the couple get sucked into conflict and end up permanently damaging their relationship. Rosie came to me saying what many divorcees tell me: I wish I had found your page when I was going through my divorce. She had no idea what was going on, and her lawyer and her ex's lawyer took advantage of her lack of understanding by dragging out what could have been a low-conflict, cheap, and fast divorce. Rosie ended up having to declare bankruptcy and live on food stamps for months, and she and her two children had to move back in with her parents. She regretted not having hired a divorce coach to guide her through the process, explain thoroughly her options, and help her handle the emotions that eventually cost her almost everything.

Rosie had been married for nine years. She fell into what I call the Who Did I Marry? group: people who fell hard during the flirting and courting phase, married quickly without truly knowing each other, and soon found out they were not compatible. They were now trapped in a marriage they did not want to be part of but felt they could not end it without bringing shame and disgrace to their lives. With time, tensions began to grow as they wanted to do things completely differently, and when the kids came along, it all became too much. They could not agree on how the kids would be raised, and any intimacy ended after the second child was born.

Although conflict kept escalating, they hoped they could stay together by taking time away from each other. Soon enough, they were doing "tag parenting," where they would take turns looking after the children and spend the rest of the time apart, only exchanging words to figure out logistics or to argue. After years of living in that hostile environment, Rosie decided she could not take it anymore and told her spouse she wanted a divorce. As it often happens, despite the fact that both partners were dissatisfied and fully aware they were not a good match, he rejected the idea. He admitted he did not love her and that they would never get along, but getting a divorce was way too expensive, complicated, and shameful for him to bear. He suggested instead they remain married but live in separate rooms and lead separate lives.

Rosie was not happy about this plan, but after several failed attempts to convince him on getting a divorce, she gave in. Again, this is a common scenario that seems harmless enough but is way more dangerous than most people anticipate. It is often relatively smooth until one of the partners gets a new lover, and then trouble begins. In their case, Rosie was hurt that he had found someone just a few months after their cohabitation/separation had begun. Arguments started to become a daily occurrence to the point that Rosie finally demanded a divorce. This time, he agreed, but they had unknowingly set the groundwork for a contentious divorce now that new negative emotions had crept in, namely jealousy and disappointment.

When Rosie found a lawyer who validated the outrage she was feeling and told her how she could get even in the divorce, she jumped into the process headfirst. The lawyer said she would get full custody, most of their assets, child support, and alimony. She could not wait to sign the retainer. But sometimes a lawyer's promises are the same as a politician's. Once you have given them the vote or the check, they give you the reality check. In Rosie's case, in order to get anything close to all her demands, she and her ex would have to spend a long time negotiating, and if he did not agree—which he would not because it was a total lose/win case—they would go to court. This could be a very long and expensive battle with no guarantees the judge would rule in Rosie's favor. But as any good shark lawyer would do, he promised her he was willing to fight to get her the justice she deserved; she just had to keep on paying his invoices.

I wish I could tell you Rosie's story had a happy ending, but sadly, it did not. This is a cautionary tale that she asked me to publish so others would be able to avoid making her mistakes. Rosie ended up spending almost $47,000 in legal and court fees. She spent two and a half years in agony, with painful back-and-forth negotiations that went nowhere and a difficult court hearing where she did not get the justice she was hoping for.

She did confess to me later that looking back, there was no justice needed. Her ex had done nothing wrong by starting a new relationship once they had separated. Rosie simply got overwhelmed by jealousy and a feeling of betrayal. If she had been coached and guided properly, Rosie might have processed and integrated her emotions and would not have been easy prey for her unscrupulous lawyer. Their divorce could have been a much different story and the long-lasting consequences could have been avoided.

The Holistic Divorce

I wished there had been a "Divorce School" when I was going through mine. There was plenty of information out there, but it was so overwhelming and complex that I felt more confused than educated. When you are considering divorce, you are already in a state of emotional duress that makes researching and analyzing legal and emotional information almost impossible. I needed a teacher, a guide who could simplify the terms, help me figure out the next steps, and coach me on techniques to deal with the emotions of divorce.

It is shocking how much confusion there is about divorce options. I find it mind-blowing that we have come up with hundreds of different diets to suit each body type and lifestyle, yet with divorce, we think "one size fits all." I am not the type to sit and complain about what is wrong with the world and then do nothing to fix it. My organization Divorce for Love is the solution I created for anyone who wants to avoid suffering the Old-School Divorce and access the information and support needed. My methodology around Holistic

Divorce is my attempt to create a new divorce option where both your emotional and logistical needs are taken into consideration.

The Holistic Divorce proposes that divorce is far from being a traumatizing event and instead can be a catalyst for positive transformation and evolution. It has the potential to encourage tremendous spiritual growth, showing how strong, capable, and resourceful you truly are. And if you lack those qualities, it has the potential to give them to you. Divorce is not the end of your life but the end of a partnership that does not work anymore and the beginning of another glorious chapter. If you learn to take control of the process and not let emotions dictate the outcome, you may end your marriage in a manner you can be proud of and move forward without emotional baggage.

When you opt into a Holistic Divorce, you are going to handle both the emotional and logistical sides with equal effort. In the past, we have relegated the entire process to a lawyer and let their legal expertise dictate how the transition will evolve and all the terms for the final agreements. With a more holistic approach, you consider the emotions of divorce and their management as a vital factor that will determine the outcome of negotiations and settlements. The history of your marriage and how your relationship shaped you will be emotionally processed so you are not left with emotional baggage. The ending of your marriage will honor all the parts of you that have been transformed during your time together, and you will not be left to integrate this powerful emotional journey on your own. With the help of a Holistic Divorce Coach or with the appropriate materials, you can learn to regulate and manage the multifaceted feelings and beliefs that play a vital role in the degree of conflict in your divorce and post-divorce life.

The Holistic Divorce directs couples toward a collaborative

dissolution whenever possible. Even if your partner refuses to commit to an amicable process, you can avoid instigating or participating in their attempts to bring you into costly litigation. Most people are reasonable enough to understand that ruining their life in order to inflict pain on their ex is simply not worth it. If they are not, you will be given the tools to help them understand how their anger and the need for revenge will play out against them long term.

In the Holistic Divorce paradigm, we accept there are many reasons to justify wanting to go separate ways. We are not bound by the need to blame the ending of the marriage on one of the partners. It is accepted that most relationships are not meant to last forever, and divorce does not have to be a bitter battle. The emphasis goes beyond elaborating on the reasons why the marriage is dissolving and focuses on how to use the ending of the relationship as a catalyst for empowerment and personal evolution.

The biggest shift the Holistic Divorce offers is a departure from a highly disputed and unnecessarily traumatic, litigious experience to an inclusion of the human need to be seen, heard, and understood through an individualized approach that inevitably reduces the chance of irreconcilable disagreements. The current situation worldwide is creating a dismantling of old structures to give way to new and improved ways to solve problems. We are acknowledging the important repercussions of disregarding our mental health, and more people are approaching therapists to overcome difficult situations and emotions. To navigate the treacherous waters of divorce, a new classification of professional coaches is emerging—The Holistic Divorce Coach.

The Holistic Divorce Coach is the professional guiding hand that will support you not just through the emotional roller coaster that is divorce but also the legal, complex maze few are capable of understanding on their own. The Holistic Divorce Institute I founded is my answer to fulfilling the increasing demand for professionally trained and certified coaches who, instead of preying on the vulnerabilities of those going through divorce, offer unbiased and scientifically proven methodologies to facilitate this transition. They are trained in modalities that range from neuroscience, Emotional Freedom Techniques (EFT), subconscious reprogramming, emotional intelligence, and quantum healing, to practical techniques in conscious communication, negotiation, and boundary setting. Beyond explaining the legalities and helping you create a strategic plan to achieve all your goals, a Holistic Divorce Coach holds the space to witness the unfolding of your story and the beliefs that have gotten you to where you are. They can assist you further in creating the life you want for yourself through visualization, journaling, and rituals created to energetically complete this cycle and move you to your next great chapter unencumbered.

I believe the time for a better divorce is here, and if ending your marriage is a possibility, stand with this revolutionary approach to avoid the endless suffering traditional divorce creates. You are most likely to go through divorce only once. I encourage you to choose to grow through it with a Holistic Divorce and the invaluable assistance of a Holistic Divorce Coach. Your future self and your children will thank you.

Martha's Divorce Story

Martha's divorce falls into the category divorce coaches call the "Gray Divorce"—a divorce for people ages fifty and up. When I began my coaching career, I didn't understand why the Gray Divorce label existed. After working with several over-fifty women, I now understand the need for a specialized approach to their divorce journey. They are a different generation and usually have a unique programming toward marriage and divorce.

The stigma of divorce is universal to everyone I work with, but it has a deeper grip on previous generations who grew up in a time when divorce was almost nonexistent and never pleasant. Besides the moral and societal pressure to remain married in order to preserve the foundation of the American Dream, there was a tremendous lack of financial independence for women and insurmountable difficulties finding a suitable partner post-divorce. Also, let's not forget that up until the 1970s, there was no option for a no-fault divorce.

Prior to the advent of no-fault divorce, a divorce was handled through an adversarial system as a civil action. A divorce could be obtained only through showing fault of one (and only one) of the parties in a marriage. One spouse had to allege the other had committed adultery, abandonment, felony, or other similarly wrongful acts. The other spouse could then plead a variety of defending arguments, such as recrimination, self-defense, or domestic abuse. Under this legal framework, one party had to lose for the other to win. It's no wonder the process left people with a bitter taste and lighter wallets.

Martha found my Instagram account through her daughter, who was contemplating divorce. When Martha's daughter told her she and her spouse may consider marriage therapy, Martha found herself repeating all the programming she had grown up with about marriage: You made vows you must keep. Your kids will be devastated. You will be alone forever. Nobody is truly happy in their marriage; you just put up with it, and so on.

Martha told me she felt like she was having an out-of-body experience as she rattled off all the nonsense she no longer believed. Martha came back into her body when she said out loud what she had been holding back for years. She told her daughter to suck it up and stay in her unhappy marriage no matter what because that was what *she* was doing. Her daughter was shocked to hear her parents had been living separate lives under the same roof for the last seven years. She knew her parents were not affectionate, that they had completely different hobbies, and that they had begun taking holidays apart because they realized compromising for every vacation meant no one was ever happy.

When Martha's daughter asked how her parents could live parallel lives under the same roof, Martha explained that this was normal among her friends. Most of them had stopped being intimate with their partners decades ago. She had also witnessed some of her braver friends getting destroyed by costly and traumatic divorces. Martha explained that the Hollywood ideal of romantic love that never dies was nothing but a bunch of lies. She had only seen and experienced love that inevitably turned into nothing more than a logistical arrangement used to have kids and advance in life. Martha told her daughter, "If you are lucky, you will reach a point when the love transforms into a friendly relationship, or at least a civilized and bearable one." Some of her most "progressive" friends had managed to find new lovers and felt like they were twenty all over again, all while remaining in their "pretend marriages." Why bother with a complicated divorce when you could have it all?

Her daughter's shock was written all over her face. All of a sudden, Martha felt a surge of shame. The plan she and most of her friends had resigned to seemed somehow terribly flawed when spoken out loud to someone of a different generation. Martha feared her daughter was disappointed—or even disgusted—by what now seemed like a coward's way of living life. Her daughter was gracious enough to hold back on giving her unsolicited advice, but she suggested Martha read some of my work and find out if she could see divorce as a better option than an unspoken agreement to remain in an unhappy marriage forever.

When Martha contacted me, she confessed that although she loved my philosophy around divorce, she did not see women her age being able to recreate such a positive experience, and most importantly, the post-divorce life I helped my clients achieve. I told her I understood her hesitation, and I could not back up my results with a testimonial that fit her profile. At that point, I had not handled any Gray Divorces. I suggested we change the paradigm and work together to prove it could be done. She was still very concerned; she wasn't convinced divorce was necessarily what she needed, and she was not excited about paying for a coach to achieve something she was not sure she even wanted.

As part of giving back to the Universe, God, or whatever you want to call it, I made a promise to myself that as long as time and finances allowed, I would accept what I call my "pro-love clients." These are like the pro bono cases lawyers take on out of principle. I told Martha she could be part of my one-on-one, eight-week coaching program for a Holistic Divorce, completely for free. Although I prepare my clients for divorce both emotionally and logistically, I would be happy to lean more into the "should I stay or go?" part of the program, and Martha and I would go in whatever direction she wanted to. Divorce was not our ultimate goal; her happiness was.

In our first session, we did a visualization exercise that has helped previous clients make up their mind and minimize the chance for second-guessing that choice. Although Marth got a clear

answer, she immediately jumped to the learned response of bury-
ing our own intuition so deep that outside voices inevitably drown
our real desires. Martha convinced herself that although she knew
divorce and the chance to love again were the path to happiness,
she did not need to be *that* happy. Being comfortable and not rock-
ing the boat were the "sensible" options for a woman her age with
no financial independence.

Most of my clients start the program with that same belief—even
women in their early thirties feel they are too old to find love again!
By week three, we have replaced every single one of their limiting
beliefs with empowering ones. Having a few extra decades of holding
onto those beliefs made it harder for Martha to dissolve them, but
I was not worried because we were not working against the clock.
We had plenty of time to remove limiting beliefs, process emotions,
and get to the logistical part of divorce that makes my clients so anxious. Martha was in no hurry to start strategizing a divorce she kept
talking herself out of, and I was so fascinated by her Herculean resistance that I had to dig deeper into my coach's toolbox. I was faced
with one of the paradoxes of my job: how to respect my client's free
will while minimizing the chance of regret with those decisions.

One of the guiding principles of my coaching philosophy is that
I do not remove a belief, no matter how toxic or counterproductive,
unless you desire to do so. I am not here to indoctrinate people on
how to live life, but I do want everyone to make decisions from their
heart and not their mind. My objective was not to show Martha how
great her life would be if she divorced because that would never be
true if subconsciously, she was holding on to the program of shame
and failure. I wanted Martha to unearth what she wanted to do with
her life if nobody would judge her decision. Whatever her soul wanted to do, I would support her unconditionally. Martha joked that I

was a terrible divorce coach if the finished product wasn't a divorce decree. A happy human is all I care about, married, divorced or in a romantic relationship with avocados. Happy people create a world worth living in. Miserable ones spread their pain to everyone, their children included, and we go on and on with generational wounding.

Martha thoroughly enjoyed our sessions and getting to know herself for the first time in her fifties. I went through a similar process in my late thirties as my pleasant marriage was disintegrating, and I had to figure out who Olga was. Not the mother, the spouse, and the businesswoman—the woman who had inhabited my body for decades with no clue of what my purpose, wants, and needs were. Over eight sessions, Martha and I did the Inner Work of a lifetime, and Martha went the extra mile by taking every exercise and learning the neuroscience behind it, reading every book recommendation, and implementing every emotional intelligence technique. Martha was aligning with her own soul, and she was glowing. Her friends thought she'd had plastic surgery, gone on a diet, or, ironically, found a lover. Martha had found herself and fallen in love with the inner guidance that her intuition provided. She reconnected with the parts of herself that we are told die with age, but if you know how to access them correctly, they actually blossom as we mature: her joy for life, a humorous approach to setbacks, the perseverance that comes from having gone through some rough patches, and a wisdom that is beyond this lifetime.

As our last session approached, seeing how far Martha had come reminded me of the reason I went into life coaching. My mentor thought I was crazy to focus on divorce. As opposed to helping people make light transformations full of positivity, helping people through divorce can involve a rather painful process. Before people reach their peak, they have to go through many valleys, creating more challenging work for their coach. However, having lived through it myself, I could not let another person navigate the uncharted territory of divorce alone. We should unconditionally support anyone going through divorce, no matter how painful it can be to witness. I teach all my coaches techniques to ensure that no matter how dark and disturbing their client's situation is, they are able to serve while protecting their own sanity.

For our last session, I was going to give Martha a few more techniques, when she surprised me with a question: "So, are we starting my eight-week program to a Holistic Divorce or what?" She told me our work had opened up her intuition and made it impossible to go back to her old life that felt so out of alignment. Martha was no longer scared about what people would say. Instead, she wanted to be an inspiration to all her friends. She wanted to help them break free from the chains of their own self-imposed prisons and was willing to trust me to lead her on the journey to her next great chapter.

Martha is now happily divorced and living closer to the water in Florida with her boyfriend, who she found in the dance class she joined after our very first session. By the way, I worked with three of her closest friends, who went on to have civilized and low-conflict divorces too. In my practice, I now call Gray Divorce "Great Divorce."

Sometimes You Have To Break From Your Marriage So Your Marriage Does Not Break You

Society is finally waking up to the idea that staying in an unhappy marriage at all costs is not beneficial for any of the parties involved, children included. Many of my clients resist this emerging truth and have a hard time letting go of the misconception that this unjustifiable sacrifice is needed. We have been indoctrinated with the concept that marriage is a never-ending compromise—which I agree with, to some extent—but when mental health and fulfillment are at stake, it is time to reconsider.

Fortunately, the messaging is shifting, and we are now seeing the spread of positive and uplifting messages about divorce and post-divorce life. The narrative of The Old-School Divorce is being replaced with the Holistic Divorce ethos—understanding that just because a marriage ends, it does not mean it was a failure. It is now proven that kids are less affected by divorce but by high-conflict environments, which can happen in married households. The unnecessary shame and guilt-tripping of divorce is being replaced by fully supportive friends and family as you break away from anything that is breaking your soul, marriage included.

I do wonder about the possibility that contrary to popular belief, we are not meant to stay in our first marriage forever. For many couples, their first marriage is the learning ground where they develop their interrelationship skills. That marriage helps them complete a phase of life when they are still learning who they are and what they want. They get to know themselves deeply and learn how to communicate with their partner better. Or not. Maybe they do not experience any growth whatsoever and instead make all the mistakes possible in the most intimate of settings. They learn what they do not want and how incredibly quickly bad communication, lack of boundary-setting, and resentment can erode love and connection. Hopefully, their first marriage turns out to be the schooling they needed, and they don't repeat the same mistakes in consequent relationships.

We cannot ignore the fact that raising children as we are trying to succeed financially—or simply making ends meet—adds extra layers of stress to what might already be a strained bond. We are not taught how to navigate disagreements, diffuse conflict, eliminate ego battles, and remove resentment from past incidents, and we attempt to maintain a commitment without the knowledge and experience to succeed at it. A lack of education on the ebb and flow of the evolution of relationships leaves many unprepared for the difficult times all marriages encounter. If we are not able to find the guidance and resources to turn these difficult phases around, we might not find our way back to the love we once shared.

All these factors combined make a powerful case for my proposal that first marriages almost do not stand a chance of survival for the majority of couples. Add to this our longer life expectancy, the rapid pace for societal changes, women's access to financial independence, and a collective raise in consciousness translating into spiritual growth that might differ from our partners, and the skyrocketing rates of divorce make perfect sense. The only question that remains is: will you break away from an arrangement that no longer feeds your soul, or will you break your soul to obey outdated conditioning?

Veronica's Divorce Story

I was so hesitant to take Veronica as a client because she had so much going on that I thought a divorce could wait until she had processed all the turmoil. Her mother, who was also her best friend, had recently passed away after a painful battle with cancer. Two months after her mother's death, Veronica was diagnosed with ovarian cancer herself, and her three-year-old was beginning to show signs of autism. She contacted me at the beginning of her medical leave to start chemo, and I wanted to tell her to wait until she was done with the treatments before even considering divorce.

I presumed her thinking was clouded with all the recent events, that she was not making rational decisions, and that I could not in good conscience accept her as a client if I felt she was not ready for the transformation. But before I could email her back to tell her to wait, I felt an intuitive hit that Veronica was ready. Ending her marriage was the win she needed to move past all the pain she was feeling. It was not my place to judge what was best for her. She was a grown woman who knew what she needed, and she was smart enough to find the right help to get her there. As soon as we had our first coaching call, my intuition was confirmed.

Veronica told me that just as her mother was passing away, she expressed deep sadness about all the things she had not done in life. Veronica presumed she was talking about "bucket list" types of regrets and was shocked to hear her mom's biggest regret was not leaving her husband when she found out about a secret affair Veronica knew nothing about. Her mother was convinced that the painful betrayal she felt had stuck to her body and turned into cancer, and she wondered if life would have been different if instead of forgiving him out of fear, she had left a marriage in which she did not feel cherished and respected.

While Veronica was distraught to hear the news, she was even more disturbed about the uncanny timing of its arrival, as only a few weeks earlier, she had caught her own husband red-handed in a spicy text exchange with a coworker with whom he was having an affair. She had not shared this with her mom because she was already going through so much suffering but also because she had no idea what she was going to do about it. As soon as she saw the texts, she wanted to tell him, "We're done. We haven't been happy for a while, and this is proof that we're not meant to be together. Let's do the right thing and end this marriage so we don't have to go behind each other's backs to get what our marriage can no longer provide."

But then, Veronica looked at her three-year-old boy sleeping in his room and resolved that before she even mentioned divorce, she and her husband should try and work things out for their son. Maybe they could go to marriage therapy or couple's counseling, or even take a trip together to see if they could fall back in love. They did all the things: they engaged in marriage therapy and individualized counseling, and they talked about taking a trip but frankly, neither of them truly wanted to. It was another thing to check off the list of "we tried everything" before giving up.

It was then that Veronica's mom was diagnosed with stage 4 breast cancer, and Veronica put everything on hold to help her go through chemo and surgery. She had not given her marital troubles much more thought until the moment when her mom disclosed her own husband's infidelity. Her mom passed away only a few days after that conversation, and just as Veronica was deep in the sadness of losing her mother—her best friend—she was diagnosed with ovarian cancer after her yearly checkup showed cancerous cells. Her oncologist suggested she undergo surgery, radiotherapy, and chemo, which was too much for Veronica to handle, given the state she was in. Her husband did show up for her in unexpected ways, but she could not figure out if it was out of love, or guilt about the affair. Either way, her mom's words stuck with her, and she did not want to go through whatever time she had left to live with regret.

Veronica sent me a DM, telling me that my Instagram page was one of her favorite ways to daydream about a better future. I made divorce seem attainable, and she found hope in my stories about building my dream home in Maui with my second husband, whom I love and adore. She wanted to get a divorce, and she understood by reading my posts that the best time to hire me would be before she even had the initial conversation with her spouse. She was sure he would cooperate, and they would have a low-conflict divorce, but she wanted to work with me because she wanted to shift quickly into her next great chapter. She had no time to waste and wanted to do all the necessary Inner Work to release her marriage and feel at peace.

Working with Veronica was one of the most beautiful experiences of my coaching career. I was amazed at her strength and courage to push forward with such radical change at an already difficult point in her life. She was determined to live a life based on her wants and desires, not society's expectations. Having confronted both death and regret, she was convinced her cancer was the direct result of not being true to herself, and she was done literally killing herself (her words). She learned to communicate with her spouse in such a way that he was able to respect her wishes and work toward a civilized and fast divorce. Every initial disagreement was quickly negotiated when we got to the root of the blockage so we could remove it and reach a final settlement in less than four months. The part I loved the most was how ready she was to absorb a new philosophy on life. Setting boundaries and teaching people pleasers to love themselves first is usually an uphill battle and takes several sessions to shift, but Veronica learned remarkably fast.

Veronica implemented all her new behaviors immediately, and she found her voice, which she used to make her doctors respect her opinion and choices. She made up her mind that surgery was enough to remove cancer from her body and refused the radio and chemo treatments. She opted instead to focus on her nutrition, fitness, and spirituality. She pursued holistic approaches until she reached an all-clear from her doctors. She is happily divorced, healthy, and has a formal relationship with her ex, which is good enough for her. She realized during marriage therapy she did not even like him as a person, and if it was not for their son, she would never want to see him again. She is dating a wonderful man who is on board with her healthy lifestyle, and having gone through divorce himself, he has learned how to be in a conscious partnership.

The Fulfilled Marriage Syndrome (FMS)

One thing that is not openly talked about regarding marriage is how passion and excitement aren't the only things that can diminish over time. Our willingness to stay—even if there is nothing fundamentally wrong with the partnership—can wane as well. When I began coming out of the "I do not want to be married" closet, I was offered conflicting advice, psychological analysis, and medication to "cure" my discontent. After many puzzled looks from friends and relatives who could not understand why I wanted to leave my wonderful husband, I realized people needed a label, almost like a scientific explanation for something they could not comprehend. So I went ahead and jokingly coined the term Fulfilled Marriage Syndrome, or FMS for short. Once I began describing my "condition" under that pseudo-medical term, the confused looks and concerned remarks faded, and communication flowed where before there was only judgment.

The only prerequisite for the FMS diagnosis is that you do the Inner Work that will give you a stronger sense of self and determine whether you are dissatisfied with your marriage or with your life in general. Inner Work is one of the most challenging tasks humans face, which is exactly why most people choose to ignore it. It involves self-examination, raising your consciousness, discovering your commanding patterns, rearranging subconscious beliefs, and awakening to your purpose. It can take a long time to accomplish, and in some cases, it will require counseling, coaching, or some form of external assistance. From there, a final decision can be made about whether to continue in the relationship or move on.

Many of the individuals suffering from FMS were raised in families and societies that consider it crucial to remain married regardless of feelings. I find it ironic that in the evolution of marriage, we have moved from a very practical arrangement to ensure survival to an over-romanticized affair where we only marry out of feelings of never-ending love and longing for each other. Yet if those feelings disappear, we are instructed to ignore their absence and keep trudging along with business as usual. The result is a pandemic of people feeling trapped in their marriages and wishing to escape before they make their lives and their loved ones miserable. Yet many do not escape because they fear the consequences.

We have pushed ourselves into a corner where we only accept the ending of a marriage if the relationship has turned into a destructive force in our life. More often than not, we change our feelings to reconcile them with our role in the marriage. We disregard our needs in favor of preserving the union at all costs. There was nothing wrong with me or my husband. I simply felt we had outgrown the marriage, and staying in it created an anxiety and unhappiness that was not in alignment with our life goals. I wish more people were honest about their own relationships. It would get us out of the maze of confusion and darkness we immerse ourselves in when we think we are being inadequate while everyone else is thriving. Getting reassurance that

I was not crazy for wanting something else and that my feelings were valid and shared by others definitely helped me keep my sanity.

Not being honest about our relationships can lead to the dangerous widespread way many people deal with dissatisfaction: through medication, especially antidepressants, which are handed out like cotton candy to women who feel disconnected in their marriages. Surely, you do not need me to tell you how we should avoid getting to this stage and how unsustainable the whole medication arrangement is. Let's stop asking people to deny and suppress their feelings and give them instead the support to thrive in whatever status they choose, married or not. What if we were encouraged to live according to our purpose and let our relationships exemplify our commitment to grow, rather than settle and die while still alive? If that means your marriage is fulfilled and has to end, let it end. What if we, as an enlightened society, accepted the following new mindset:

You have permission to leave: you will not be criticized; your integrity will not be judged. Instead, society will fully support and accept your decision.

Cindy's Divorce Story

Cindy's story is a perfect example of the Fulfilled Marriage Syndrome, which I believe is the type of divorce that will become more commonplace. After being happily married to a sweet and understanding man for thirteen years, Cindy began feeling the uneasiness around reaching forty. When she came to me, she diagnosed herself with what society calls a "midlife crisis." After I went through my own, I renamed it "Midlife Arises" because in my opinion, far from being a low point in our existence, this is the launching pad to great-ness if we are willing to go through it.

Midlife Arises might feel like a "dark night of the soul," but it is actually a blessing. We get to reconsider whether our lives are a re-flection of our ideals or someone else's before we are on our deathbed and there is nothing we can do to escape our regrets. As challenging as the transformation might be, it is inevitable, especially if you have lost yourself or your dreams on the journey toward adulthood. Most people will experience Midlife Arises if they go through a life-threat-ening disease or another traumatic event that forces them to ana-lyze whether they are living life according to their own compass.

Divorce can be considered one of those transformational mo-ments when you get to recalibrate and reconnect to your dreams and who you want to be. Unfortunately, society insists on making divorce a traumatic event with only negative consequences, but I disagree, and my client's stories prove divorce can be the catalyst to the life you are truly meant to live. Cindy had to overcome this lim-iting belief before she could make peace with the fact that her rela-tionship had run its course, and there was no need to add shame or failure to this fact.

I could completely relate to Cindy's anxiety about ending her marriage to someone who, by everybody's standards, was "as good as they get." Divorcing a person who is being nasty to you is hard because of all the resentment and pain you have to endure, but di-vorcing a nice guy can be just as challenging. You will find yourself buried in guilt and remorse for what you perceive as an unnecessary, painful transition for you and your family. And it is easy to get stuck in the desperation of wanting to be free from a golden cage but to also be afraid of never finding anything better. Cindy was convinced she could live a dissatisfied life in a marriage that lacked intimacy and love but existed in the realm of comfort and friendship. Their marriage was characterized by the FMS pattern of being roommates more than lovers. Their parenting had turned into "tag parenting," and dreams about the future were postponed until their three kids would leave for college (another nine years). Then, Cindy figured, would be a good time to divorce, so the kids would not be affected, and she would still be young enough to survive by herself.

I respect all my clients' limiting ideas of "I'm too old, too broke, too codependent, or too attached to my kids" as reasons to keep their logical minds satisfied. However, their hearts do not abide by date of birth or a number in the bank account. Their hearts know the root of their addictions and can override them. It understands that the parent-child bond goes beyond the need for constant contact and that this is only an excuse to avoid facing their fear of loneliness. When presented with the suggestion that someone stays in an unhappy relationship, no matter how full of hostility or disagreements it is, I always ask them to do a little math exercise for me: Multiply the years that they have to wait (for their kids to leave, their career to get better, their parents to pass away, whatever the case may be) by 365. Do a little visualization of whatever their current reality is, and replicate it to every single day the calculation offered. Sit with the feeling that number creates, then tell me if you can honestly go through with it. Most of my clients realize they have been lying to themselves and that sooner or later, they will not be able to take it anymore. They are simply postponing the inevitable.

After Cindy's discovery call, it was clear she was holding onto the fantasy that she could wait for her kids to leave. She kept reminding me it was only going to be nine more years, and her husband was a good guy, so it would be OK. I asked her if she wanted me to send her a visualization exercise I offer to all my clients to help them figure out if they should stay or go. She graciously agreed, but I was not sure which version of Cindy would do the exercise—the one who knew she wasn't happy or the one who was living in denial—because ignorance is bliss, especially when it comes to feelings we do not want to feel. I was not surprised when she replied to my follow-up email with a polite "thank you, but no thank you" as she would not be needing coaching because she was going to stay in the marriage. I made a note in my calendar to reach back out in six months and see how things were going. A few weeks before my calendar sent me a reminder to reach out, Cindy sent me a direct message on Instagram. She couldn't take it anymore. For Cindy and her husband, the previous few months had felt like living inside a pressure cooker, and what used to be a pleasant enough situation had quickly turned sour. She grew restless as she witnessed one of her best friends, who had divorced a year ago, falling madly in love with an amazing man who adored her. What used to be whispers of a better life somewhere else became screams that kept her up all night.

Cindy had been relying heavily on sleeping pills and a few too many glasses of wine during the day to calm her anxiety and put a stop to arguments. Yet her subconscious mind—the part of her that craved the freedom and joy her friend was experiencing—kept sabotaging every interaction with her husband and turning each one into conflict. A new feeling had added itself to her array of negative emotions: regret at trying to avoid the inevitable and now finding herself in a precarious situation. When we first talked less than half a year ago, their relationship was civilized and pleasant enough. They acted as roommates but still attended all events together, and only the people closest to them were aware of their marital problems.

Now, things were drastically different. They had been arguing nonstop, Cindy found 99 percent of his habits extremely irritating, and she admitted that although he had not changed much, she could no longer recognize the man with whom she had fallen in love. She was annoyed by his presence and could only find flaws and faults in everything he did. She knew she was being unreasonable but could not help blaming her husband for not loving her like the new boyfriend loved her friend. When I asked Cindy if she loved her husband the way her friend loved her newfound partner, she quietly said no, and in that moment, she realized she might have been pointing fingers at the wrong suspect.

I offered Cindy my favorite marriage analogy: it is like a car. There are some people who have old classics that look spotless and run like a dream, but that does not happen by chance. They invest every penny and spare minute into making them look spiffy. There are only a handful of those passionate car enthusiasts. The majority of us use our cars whichever way we were taught, maybe taking care of them, or maybe carelessly scratching and bumping them constantly. Some cars are kept in good condition on the exterior but have been neglected on the inside and eventually start breaking down. It might take extra effort to get them back to working order, or the damage might be so deep that we can't get it back on the road, and it has to be taken to the junkyard. Cindy was at the point where her car could not be restarted, but even if it could, she was so disappointed and jaded by it that she wouldn't want to drive it anymore anyway. Instead of fighting the inevitable, we had to work on validating Cindy's emotions to help her move onto her next chapter.

I know some of you might be terribly offended that I'm comparing the sacred institution of marriage to a vehicle and suggesting that if it stops working, you can go and get yourself a new one. Please understand, I am not trying to undermine the institution of marriage—but I do want to remove the insane amount of guilt that exists around the natural instinct of simply wanting more, something better and more aligned with who you are. It is very likely you are a completely different person from who you were when you married all those years ago, and that is OK.

We have created an absurd amount of criticism and judgment around a basic human need for improvement and growth in the name of a contract that, let me remind you once again, *can be legally dissolved.* It is just our morals and flawed conditioning that keeps us stuck in a paradigm that does not work for most. Instead of trying to fit yourself into a mold that only a few are meant to exist in, ask yourself: Is this relationship helping me grow? Is it making me a better person? Am I learning valuable lessons to become the best version of myself? If the answer is no, and you know there is no space for the relationship to become the grounds where you can flourish, then it is time to let it go, no matter how hard your logical mind fights it.

Cindy's rationale was in line with what most of society buys into: if her spouse was not abusive, hurtful, or unfaithful, the best thing was to stay put. Do not rock the boat, suck it up like your parents and their parents did, and do not disturb the status quo. However, our world has changed dramatically, and those beliefs that were once easy to believe are being dismantled rapidly. Cindy was the perfect example of how much harder it is to live by that flawed system. She had her own income from a job that made her feel appreciated and valued. She had a rich network of other high achievers who were always looking for ways to improve their lives, learn new skills, and explore new adventures. Her kids were just as close to her as they were to their dad, who, because he worked from home, had spent a large portion of his time with them. They were also getting to the ages where they needed their parents less and less, being two full teenagers and a self-sufficient nine-year-old. None of them were troubled kids, and they had maintained a great dynamic, despite the issues in their parents' marriage. Cindy felt confident they could all continue with the family traditions and maintain a friendly relationship post-divorce. By this point, what worried her more was jeopardizing the family dynamic by staying in the marriage now that she desperately felt the need to leave.

First, we worked through Cindy's fears to leave a "nice guy." Then, we focused on how to have the conversations necessary to get him on the same page. Remember, they had agreed to stay together until the youngest went to college, but now Cindy wanted to rewrite that contract, and she was sure he would not take it well. I usually dedicate a whole session to teaching my clients how to have these vital conversations because so often, we ruin the whole divorce process by mishandling this crucial starting point. Cindy was able to calmly and peacefully convince her husband that the inevitable was happening, and it would be best if they took control of the process before their relationship was too damaged. She managed to turn him around in one conversation, which proves that with the right coaching and willingness, you can make your spouse understand the advantages of doing divorce the holistic way.

Once we overcame the biggest hurdle, everything else fell into place rather easily. I explained to Cindy all her options for a low-conflict divorce, and she agreed with her husband that they would go the collaborative route. There was almost zero animosity, and they now have a cordial post-divorce relationship, thanks to their avoidance of any nasty legal procedures and revenge settlements. I am happy to let you know that Cindy has now been divorced for two years, they have both found new partners that make them feel alive, and their children are delighted to have four loving adults and are able to see their parents laugh and be joyful again.

SETTING THE DIVORCE
RECORD STRAIGHT

⌒

As you begin considering divorce, you will likely find the beliefs society has subconsciously programmed into you are the most damaging variables wreaking havoc on the process. The completely mistaken and "politically correct" views we have held up until now are nearly entirely responsible for the stigma surrounding divorce. When one analyzes the current paradigm, this is what we have been force-fed to accept as the truth:

- Divorce is a failure.

- When you divorce, your "home sweet home" becomes a broken home.

- Children are guaranteed to be adversely affected by a divorce, and most of them will be traumatized.

- Your marriage must have been full of problems if it had to end.

- One of the partners must have done something terribly wrong.

- You are selfish because you are putting your happiness above your partner's or your children's.

Each of these beliefs are verbalized by others when you start sharing the news of your divorce, and you have to be mentally prepared to hear them. The majority of reactions will include horrified looks, shocked gasps, and heartfelt condolences. There tends to be pain and grieving during the decision-making process, but often those feelings have been resolved by the time the separation or divorce is made official. Having everybody remind you of all those heavy emotions as you are trying to move forward only makes the transition more difficult. Good boundaries, the courage to let people know what is acceptable to say or do, and not taking other people's reactions personally are all required to navigate this transition successfully.

When I work with my clients, we set the record straight with all the limiting and outdated views about divorce so we can replace them with empowering ones. This is what I call replacing the "Losing Mindset"—limiting beliefs that keep us stuck in endless litigation and prove damaging to our emotional wellbeing—with the "Winning Mindset." Let's explore different aspects of the Losing Mindset and all its erroneous beliefs and how to replace them with the Winning Mindset for a successful divorce.

The Divorce Purge

The Divorce Purge is the perceived or real loss of financial security, a plan for the future, family life, and even friends or family support.

I know the term I coined is far from sexy, but it is honestly the most accurate description for the discomfort caused by the voluntary or involuntary release of what once belonged to us. If you can get ready for the Divorce Purge with the right mindset, you will save yourself a great deal of suffering. For those who did not have the chance to prepare and are in the depths of disappointment and grieving their losses, I encourage you to search for professional help that can teach you the techniques to master the somewhat tricky process of letting go.

The first thing to remember about the Divorce Purge is that it is not personal. The universe is not conspiring to take everything away from you. This is a "Kondo'ing" of your life; like Marie Kondo, you are getting rid of what does not serve you anymore so you can make room for the abundance that is truly meant for you. Having worked through both my own journey and with my clients on the process of letting go, I realize it is not easy. Forgiveness and letting go (also known in Buddhism as "detachment") are probably two of the most challenging actions for humans. In my opinion, to fully forgive what seems unforgivable and to let go of the pain of the past is an extraordinary feat. Divorce will be your opportunity to work on these two skills so you can apply them in all areas of your life. Imagine all the suffering you can avoid when you know that no matter what people do, you can forgive and release them so their actions have no impact on you.

Society has not given us a healthy way of handling divorcing couples and their common relationships. I often joke that in the divorce settlement, there should be a section for friends' custody where you arrange who gets to keep whom from your circle and if visitation hours are allowed. There is an unspoken agreement that you cannot remain friends with both. Sides need to be chosen and enforced, especially when it comes to gatherings where it is assumed the divorced couple is incapable of sharing the same space. This might be the case for some, but the world needs to understand that divorce is becoming normalized, and the anger and bitterness of the Old-School Divorce is being replaced by mature and civilized post-divorce relationships. More people are choosing the path of collaborative divorce and learning to either maintain a friendly relationship with their ex or at least tolerate them enough to not throw knives at them at a public gathering.

My advice is twofold: First, agree with your ex about having a cordial relationship so people don't feel uncomfortable about having you both around. If you are not in the amicable spectrum, then understand that friendships will have to be redistributed. Secondly, approach every common friend you care about and explain the situation and how you would like to move forward. You do not have to contact every minor acquaintance—let those chips fall where they may. But let the people you hold close to your heart know you would like the relationship to remain. Elaborate as much or as little as you feel comfortable.

The first Winning Mindset programming I suggest you apply is:

Some things and people will go, and that is OK. Thank them for everything, but accept you are no longer meant to have them in your life.

Divorce Is One Of The Most Traumatizing Events Of Your Life

Divorce, along with losing your job and the death of a loved one, is considered one of the most traumatic events anyone can endure—

quite a devastating belief to entertain if you are considering entering divorce territory. However, the Winning Mindset says divorce is not one predetermined event but whatever you and your partner make of it. Even without your spouse's support, you can still work toward an event that is far from traumatizing and instead an empowering transformation.

I am not saying divorce is easy; even with the most collaborative of spouses and the best support you can get, it is still a challenging transition. But I'm also not saying divorce sucks, you will never recover, and you and your children will be forever damaged. I truly believe each experience is different, and you have a huge amount of control as to how it evolves. Divorce has indeed traumatized many of us, but the paradigm is changing, and our children do not have to suffer as we did.

One of the biggest misconceptions is that divorce inevitably traumatizes children. However, research has proven it is not divorce, but conflict, that causes trauma. Many children have the misfortune to live in married households that are submerged in hostility and emotional toxicity. They fare far worse than kids from households where parents divorced in a civilized manner. The one variable affecting every individual who says, "My parents' divorce was traumatizing," is how belligerent the marriage, divorce process, and life after was. Let's be honest: it's unusual that a relationship ends without a certain amount of anger, resentment, and disappointment, but it is up to us whether we turn those emotions into long-lasting conflict or short-lived discomfort.

It is fairy-tale nonsense that the most ideal conditions for a perfectly balanced and loving childhood are only possible within the confines of the marriage that brought them into the world. There is no research or empirical evidence to support the accepted belief that children are negatively affected by parents ending their marriage and living separately. And I sure as hell want to erase the belief that our unconditional love toward our children demands we sacrifice our happiness to stay in a marriage that needs to end.

One thing we must remind ourselves is that no matter how painful divorce is, it always ends, but the trauma of the unresolved suffering might stay with you forever. When experiencing trauma of any kind—physical, emotional, or mental—our bodies might go into shock while trying to shut down our conscious brains. The body is protecting us from something that is hurting us, something we may not even understand. An unfortunate coping method for trauma is avoidance. We try to suppress our feelings and reality, hoping the situation will just disappear or heal on its own. With trauma, time does not heal; it only conceals. Concealing makes the process longer and more harmful in the end. Our trauma begins to heal the moment we choose change.

No one openly talks about how staying in an unhappy marriage can be just as painful as a divorce, without any chance of ending that suffering. I have seen many people flourish after divorce, while others have stayed in unhappy marriages, only to sink into depression and substance abuse with the tremendous trauma the relationship causes for themselves and their families. I suggest you take a look at your current situation and figure out if avoiding the potential pain of divorce will compensate for a lifetime of suffering.

The second Winning Mindset programming I suggest you apply is:

If you learn how to handle the emotional roller coaster of divorce, you can be left with no scars and a whole world of possibilities for a truly fulfilling life.

You Have To Be 100 Percent Sure Before You Make This Decision

Divorce is not a decision to be made without first trying to solve whatever issues are eroding your marital happiness *and* doing the Inner Work to determine if ending the marriage is truly what needs to happen. However, I don't suggest trying every single marriage counseling option or any psychological approach if it does not resonate with you. I have seen people starting their divorce already so jaded from trying everything under the sun to resuscitate a marriage that was certainly dead. By the time they start talking about divorce, they are exhausted, bitter, and terribly upset that they put all this time into saving what they have to end now.

It is counterproductive to use all your energy in the "fixing" part, especially if one of you is already clear that the marriage will not survive. But the majority of divorced people, me included, did not have a moment when we were 100 percent sure and prepared for divorce. We knew we were "done," but just thinking about the complexities of divorce created a pressure that made us question if we could really go ahead with it. The divorce journey involves a lot of "one step forward and two steps back" shuffling. You will doubt your choices and be tempted to go back to the drawing board one more time to save the marriage. Sometimes fear will make you spiral out of control. All of this simply ends up delaying the inevitable and making it more confusing for you and your kids.

Like most major transitions in life, you are never fully prepared for what is ahead. Ask anyone who decides to have children, start a business, or move to a different country. The only difference with divorce is that we feel like we need to be 100 percent certain so when hard times hit, we do not look back and try to sabotage the process out of fear. There will be no test, quiz, or clairvoyant to give you a full guarantee that this is what is best for you. You have to believe what is ahead will be better than what you are leaving behind, then work toward creating that reality.

The third Winning Mindset programming I suggest you apply is:

When you know, you know; yet you may be terrified to accept it and will create doubt and self-sabotage until you remove those fears.

Expensive Litigation That Ends In Court Is The Only Path

Most people are shocked to hear that you do NOT need to hire a lawyer to handle your divorce or go through the court system with a judge making the final decision. It is not required by law, and often, hiring a lawyer to manage the whole process is only needed for high-conflict situations that cannot be managed with alternative dispute resolutions. These cases are the minority. If you can negotiate all the terms on your own or with the help of coaches, mediators, or lawyers, you will not have to appear in front of a judge.

Today, you can even do the whole process online, and some of these preparation services offer paralegal and legal coaching assistance. This can be the cheapest option, but it might cost you more in the long run if your agreement is not fair on both parties. I do not suggest refusing legal advice from a trusted professional. Depending on your circumstances, it might be advisable to consult with a family lawyer in your state at the beginning of the process—even before you have agreed with your spouse on getting a divorce—to learn about your legal rights, expected timelines, and what you need to know about the process ahead. You can keep consulting with them as needed without having to retain them for full counsel. Once the Marital Agreement has been drafted, you should consult again with a lawyer and never sign anything until your lawyer has reviewed the documents.

I want you to fully understand that the divorce journey can take many paths, and plenty of them do not involve a lawyer and a judge making the final decisions. The moment you hand over the entire process to lawyers, you might be entering a dangerous game where things can escalate quickly, and you can easily lose control. Fees add up fast with billable hours from both lawyers, and if your case ends up in court, you will have to agree to a settlement decided by a judge whose application of the law might differ widely from the justice you were seeking. I advise that you work with a divorce coach to tailor the best path for you in the realms of Alternative Dispute Resolution formats such as Collaborative Divorce, Mediation, Arbitration, and Online Paralegal Services.

The fourth Winning Mindset programming I suggest you apply is:

There are plenty of ways to divorce that do not involve nasty litigation. Educate yourself on what works best to keep control and stay out of court.

Your Ex Is Not Your Paycheck

There are some truths about divorce that, although painful to hear, need to be said. Rather than criticizing some beliefs or actions, I am offering an alternative view that might save you heartache. In the divorce process, we look at the financial part as two sets: first, the assets and liabilities to be divided in a fair distribution; second, the financial assistance that might be needed to support one parent for taking more custody or for having an income differential. We must not confuse divorce with a transaction where all past emotional debts are settled through the allocation of physical assets. Some unscrupulous lawyers will tell you this is possible and that they will fight to achieve this goal. They often omit the fact that the cost might exceed the amount you are requesting, and besides, there are no guarantees you will even get all the assets you seek.

I am not saying the partner who stayed home to raise the children and took time away from their career to care for the household or to fully support their spouse in advancing their career should be left with nothing. Child support and alimony, unless otherwise stated with a prenup or with an understanding and generous ex, is temporary support to help you get back on your feet, after which, you are expected to provide your own income. I want to offer some hope for those who believe they are at a great disadvantage financially, either because they stayed home to raise their children or because they produce less income than their spouse. I have witnessed many glorious transformations from clients who were at first certain they could not make it on their own, then went on to create empires, with or without child support and alimony. Today's world of online business, affiliate programs, and side hustles can turn a small stream of passive income into a cash machine that generates wealth, allowing you to stay afloat without relying on your ex.

The fifth Winning Mindset programming I suggest you apply is:

Save yourself disappointment by setting reasonable expectations. Instead of spending energy fighting to get more support, focus on creating the financial stability you crave on your own.

The Loss/Gain Game Of Divorce

We tend to focus on the negative and what we are going to lose, but what about what we stand to gain? Yes, there will be a crapload of sleepless nights, anxiety and panic attacks, confusion, and a whole roller coaster of emotions. There will also be plenty of newfound hope, courage, and a resilience that cannot be learned in theory. To focus on the positive, I encourage you to choose your thoughts and words carefully—not just for negotiations or conversations with your ex, but also with what you say to yourself. For instance, if you say, "I have lost," then your reality is one of scarcity and grief. If you say, "I have removed what does not serve me anymore," you are creating an empowered experience.

Probably the most painful adjustment (I do not call it "loss") is not having full-time access to children if you are opting for shared custody. I will be very straight and tell you that being what I call a "Full-On/Part-Time Mom" has made me the best mother I could be. Having grown up in a dysfunctional family with a mother who did not know how to nurture her children, I realized after becoming a mother myself that I had no clue how to be a loving and caring one. Many women have been raised by wounded mothers and are now hurting their kids in the same ways yet are not able to stop it.

If it had not been for my divorce, I would not have had the space I needed to do the deep and hard Inner Work to learn to mother myself so I could take care of my kids. When I am with them, I am 100 percent devoted. I can access the kind of conscious parenting I want to model for them. When they are not with me, I am at peace knowing that their dad is taking great care of them, and I am free to create the life I used to dream of and be the change I want to see in the world.

The sixth Winning Mindset programming I suggest you apply is:

Divorce will not affect your ability to be the best parent possible. Open up to the possibility that it may bring you closer to your children.

THE DIVORCE
JOURNEY

One of the biggest causes of anxiety around divorce is having no clue what to expect and what steps you are supposed to take. My clients often ask the question, "Where do I even start?" My answer is, "Start where you are." Despite differences on each individual's journey, there is a universal pattern running through most divorces. What follows is a description of the most common divorce stages to help you figure out where you are, what comes next, and how to navigate it all in a resourceful and informed manner. I also want you to be aware of what I call "The Divorce Shuffle," where you may move one stage further only to relapse two steps back. This is normal and to be expected, especially if you are not using professional help to keep you moving ahead. But do not despair—often, you just need to slow down before you can tackle the next task. Be gentle with yourself, and reach out for help if it becomes too overwhelming on your own and you need an accountability partner or coach.

STAGE 1:
Are We OK? Am I OK?

This is not when the trouble starts; this is when the problem starts being recognized. The issues in the marriage have been simmering for a while, and whether there has been open confrontation, or everything is being pushed down and ignored, there is a moment when you wonder if you are on the right path. Often, cohabitation, raising children, and the stresses of our fast-paced life are so demanding that our marriage simply disintegrates under the weight of it all, and we are completely unaware until it is too late. By the time we start wondering if our relationship is healthy, there is already a tumor growing and something needs to be done.

This is the phase some people will equate with denial in the grieving process. But this is more than denial—it is a systematic and continued justification of why things are the way they are. At this stage, we focus on normalizing the abnormal, looking for examples to prove this is the expected trajectory of marriages, as we Google if there is something wrong for not wanting to have sex with our partner. The problem is, we cannot normalize madness. The mere fact that the recurring doubts keep coming shows this not a well-evaluated and aware existence. It is the voice of your soul whispering to you: *No, sweetheart, you are not OK. This is not OK. Something has to change.*

In my opinion, this is one of the most crucial moments in life. You are confronted with the voice that sounds right inside of you but that completely clashes with society's messaging. I cannot tell you what you have to do, but I can share with you my experience and maybe inspire you to find your own path. In these pages, I will show you my process to discern which voice is yours and which is fear from cultural programming working against your evolution. Once you learn the difference, it is up to you to choose which one you will follow. In my case, no matter how much I tried to silence it, my intuition would not go away. The whispers of my soul turned into louder messages that eventually screamed for my attention. I am so happy I listened because my life following society's guidelines would have led me down a hole of quiet desperation and self-destruction.

STAGE 2:
"Come To Jesus" Moment

The denial, justification, and normalizing are not working, and you are slipping into the "Come to Jesus" moment. You are approaching the second stage: accepting what is happening. Not resisting it, not trying to fix it or medicate it away. Simply accepting that your marriage is ending, and you have a tough transition to go through before you can move on with your life. You have to accept your reality before you can change it.

Often, people compare the divorce process to the grieving one, and I will not deny the similarities. Yet grieving tends to happen after something has been lost. Divorce, on the other hand, needs your active participation to grieve what you are about to lose. Even if you are the one initiating the divorce, it does not mean you planned or expected this perceived or real loss. You will have plenty of sadness and despair to go through before you get to accept the reality of the situation. Be prepared for those emotions to accompany you in this stage as you let the waves of grief wash over you.

Some will resist this stage so hard that the universe may have to intervene. This is when we see affairs, accidents, bankruptcy, disease, or any other major event that might push your relationship past the breaking point. In 2020, coronavirus and all the other challenging events of the year acted as the strong push that threw many couples off-kilter without a chance to recover. Others going through this stage may experience a period of self-reflection and healing that accelerates their growth. However, if their partners do not take part in this transformation, they might be left behind with a gap too big to bridge. Some will simply reach their limit and realize the more they try to stay in their marriage, the harder their divorce will be. There is a point in the disintegration of a marriage when trying to save it only leads to conversations getting out of hand and both parties saying things that can't be unsaid. Such interactions open a new tab on nastiness and add disharmony to the divorce procedures that might have been avoided had they accepted their "Come to Jesus" moment.

STAGE 3:
Getting Your Spouse On Board

Even though this was one of the biggest obstacles I had to deal with during my own divorce, I did not expect this would be the first concern for 90 percent of my clients. Although we can go ahead with divorce even if our partner does not want to, I strongly recommend you try and bring them on board by using techniques from conscious communication styles. You have no idea how extremely difficult it is to reach any agreements with someone who is disgruntled and in total opposition.

The first thing we do when I face this issue with a client is dissect their partner's mindset. We paint a clear picture of what beliefs are blocking them from accepting this as an inevitable and probably necessary step. Then we discuss their "fighting style"—the way both my client and their spouse respond to anything challenging. I would love to call it "communication style," but the truth is that often, when we are presented with information we do not want to hear and decisions we do not wish to make, we tend to become confrontational and end up in conflict without a chance for conscious communication.

What I am trying to understand is: Do they disrespect your opinions? Do they block you from expressing yourself? Do they turn abusive, insult you, and criticize you for bringing up the subject? On the other end of the spectrum, can they hear you with an open mind, even though they might not change their own mind? Can they politely disagree? Do they not hold a grudge after the conversation is over?

Once all this information has been gathered, I get to work creating a strategy for the critical conversations. These conversations happen first and foremost with the spouse, then with the children, and lastly with family and friends. Because these conversations set the tone for the new relationship with your spouse, I create visualizations for my clients to rehearse before sitting down to talk, thereby leaving very little to chance. Here is a general outline of how I prepare my clients to have the conversation with their spouse:

- When you are ready to talk to your spouse about divorce, ask for permission to start the conversation. Do not just spring it upon them; instead, request a time and place, preferably in public as it helps diffuse conflict.

- Make sure they understand this is happening. Explain how you are not trying to fix it or work on the marriage anymore. You are ready for a divorce, and you both have to find a way to figure out how to do it without affecting the children and everybody's financial future.

- Learn Conscious Communication and be selective, using only words that encourage positive behaviors rather than those that reprimand for past choices.

- Avoid projecting your fears, anger, or sadness into the conversation by staying as far away from feelings as possible. Unless you are completely confident that you are capable of remaining neutral, do not mix emotions and the logistics of the divorce process.

- Maintain respect at all times. If your spouse has a tendency to insult or disrespect you, set a boundary by communicating that this is unacceptable, ask to start again with a civilized manner, and if the attacks persist, reschedule the conversation for another time.

- Observe your feelings and your partner's without judgment or reaction. See each conversation as information gathering for setting up the new ground rules in your divorce and post-divorce life.

- Communicate your needs by respectfully requesting what you need without adding emotional debts or threats.

- Listen with empathy and understanding to what your partner needs. It is crucial to recognize patterns with what your partner considers non-negotiables and the areas where there is room to negotiate.

- Be willing to make concessions, but do not disclose them right there and then—this will come later when we discuss negotiation techniques.

- Take as many time-outs as needed to create space and time to process if things are escalating. If this does not work, ask to finish the meeting for the day and reconvene at another time.

- Set boundaries: always maintain respect, never converse while angry, do not throw guilt or blame.

STAGE 4:
FOFU—Fear Of Fucking Up

Not everybody goes through this, but if you do, be aware it is a critical stage where your divorce can be kept amicable or take a nasty turn based on your fears alone. This is the point where disagreements turn into conflict due to an overwhelming fear of fucking up your life that shuts down your rational brain and forces you to adopt a combative stance. You are not just fighting with your ex but with yourself as well, second-guessing if any of this is justified, if you are just overreacting, if it would be easier to go back to therapy and marriage counseling, maybe wait until the kids are gone or the promotion at work comes through, etc. Your mind will race with all the "logical" reasons why divorce is a huge mistake and convince you that to avoid fucking up, you must retreat and abort the process.

Let me give you another perspective: What if you are not scared of fucking everything up but are terrified of what you are capable of? What if you are not afraid of how your ex will react but simply uncomfortable with conflict? Most of us are, and we tend to recoil at the prospect of disagreements that might escalate. When you are

putting your financial security, access to your children, and even social status on the table, fear will certainly make you wonder if this
is a gamble you can take. But what if instead, you learn how to communicate to de-escalate conflict? What if you learn the negotiation
techniques most successful businesspeople use? What if you develop the emotional strength and resilience to withstand any attacks
and redirect your energy toward successful resolutions?

It all depends on the partners making a decision to commit
to having a low-conflict divorce under any circumstances—*not
avoiding conflict at all costs but learning how to manage that conflict.* Even if the partner initially refuses to cooperate, I have witnessed incredible transformations when the right techniques are
employed. What you resist not only persists, but magnifies, can
become unbearable, and can explode in their face. Once they understand that, conflict can turn into a manageable negotiation with
nothing to fear—FOFU included.

> *Your goal is not avoiding conflict but managing it. This
> means anticipating, preparing, and rehearsing the outcome
> for whatever conflict is in the future.*

Conflict during divorce is often used as an excuse to hurt others
because they hurt us. Divorce is construed as the grand finale to settle all the resentments that were never properly processed during
the marriage and have become stronger than our desire to keep the
peace. When you throw the distribution of wealth and access to children into the mix, you get a recipe for disaster. You must accept the
mindset that divorce is not a process to settle emotional debts with
physical assets. Instead, aim not at being right but at generating the
only positive outcome: a favorable conclusion for both parties. No-

tice I did not say "agreement." To move from conflict to agreement, you will probably have to learn negotiation techniques as well. For now, you can be pleased if you manage to consciously speak and listen with respect, and no further damage is done. Showing goodwill and your intention to steer clear from damaging conflict will create the trustworthy environment needed for satisfactory negotiations down the road. Until we learn conflict management, we can forgive ourselves and others for allowing disagreements to escalate, then learn how to do it better next time.

STAGE 5:
Getting Professional Help

Divorce is so complex and nuanced that it is highly advisable—for both your mental health and financial protection—to find professionals to help you navigate it safely. In the past, the one and only option was to contact a lawyer and let them handle everything. Today, more people are opting to engage an entire team instead of a family lawyer to create a more holistic process. The team can include: a divorce coach, a collaborative lawyer, a mediator, a divorce financial advisor, and a therapist. This creates the best conditions for a Holistic Divorce, where emotional and logistical components are handled in conjunction to make the best decisions for everybody involved.

Divorces with the highest success rate—meaning they are most cost-effective, did not take years, and maintained a civilized relationship between the parties—tend to involve at least two of the following professionals:

- **DIVORCE COACH:** The first call to make if you are even

thinking about divorce is to a divorce coach you can trust, ideally a Holistic Divorce Coach. This is the professional who will educate you on the process, help you handle the emotions of divorce, and coach you to create the best strategy for you and your children. Because divorce coaching is an emerging profession, it can make people feel intimidated and confused at the prospect of having to work with another person beyond their lawyer. However, those who have relied on the services of a divorce coach are now the driving force for the growth of our industry. They are vocal in recommending others do the same to avoid losing control of their divorce or abandoning the whole process because they got overwhelmed and are now stuck in an unhappy marriage forever.

- **COLLABORATIVE LAWYER:** I recommend all my clients choose one of two ways to work with a lawyer: you can retain them for the whole process, or you can consult at the beginning of the process—to learn what your rights and options are—and again at the end to review all documents before you sign final agreements. You have to be careful with who you hire to represent you: some will want to fight, even if you don't, whereas others might want to make the process (as well as their billing hours) as long as possible. There are even lawyers who will take the divorce in a litigious direction when there is no need for it. However, if you opt for a collaborative process, both your lawyer and your spouse's lawyer are agreeing to stay out of court and mediate all agreements.

- **DIVORCE FINANCIAL ANALYST:** This is a professional who can help you gather all the information you need to create a financial settlement depicting your assets and liabilities and projections to cover your current and future needs. I recommend letting the professionals handle this delicate aspect instead of getting overwhelmed by all the financial disclosures, calculations, and worksheets needed for negotiations. I also appreciate the neutrality they bring to the heated subject of financial fairness.

- **MEDIATOR:** A mediator is crucial to help you negotiate with your spouse if the lines of communication have broken down. This can be a compromise between doing the whole process by yourself or handing it over solely to a lawyer. You can also use a mediator in combination with a lawyer and divorce coach to keep the cost down—by paying a lower mediator's rate than a lawyer's—and avoid the risk of escalating into litigation. Ideally, choose someone who used to be a family lawyer or judge, so they are fully versed in how the court system works. Most importantly, choose someone with whom both parties feel completely at ease. You can even do mediation online, which allows you to pick the absolute best fit possible, even if they are not located nearby.

- **THERAPIST:** If you feel like you need extra emotional support that goes beyond the scope of your divorce coach, I recommend individualized therapy. It might also be necessary to remove some of the emotional damage done during the marriage, especially if it was an abusive relationship. Also, consider having your kids see a therapist if you are in a high-conflict divorce or they are struggling with the changes.

You do not have to use all these professionals. It all depends on the complexity of your case and how much help you need in each area. But avoid the mistake of not hiring them at all because you think you will be saving money. You might end up paying way more for a worse end result if you are not employing the right person for each aspect of the process. If you truly need a financial advisor but instead ask your lawyer to handle those issues, you might, depending on your lawyer's expertise, end up paying a much higher hourly rate and not collecting all the right information or analyzing it in the right manner. Ultimately, not getting a clear financial picture of your assets and liabilities might cost you in child support, alimony, and the final distributions of the settlement.

The same idea applies to not using a divorce coach and instead getting misinformation from friends and relatives. When you get legal advice that does not match your goals, you risk ending up in court. Alternatively, you could work with a divorce coach who will explain all your options, guide you to the best strategy, and ensure your emotions are handled outside of the lawyer's room so the negotiations keep moving along. I predict that in the near future, divorce coaches will be the leaders in the divorce process, helping their clients navigate the emotional and logistical parts while coordinating all the other professionals involved.

STAGE 6:
Letting Kids, Relatives, And Friends Know

By this stage, you are hopefully working with a divorce coach who can help you strategize the process, learn about conscious communication, and learn how to let your children, friends, and relatives know what is happening. Oftentimes these people already know or suspect what is happening; other times, it is completely new information, and a professional divorce coach can help you create the best script for each situation.

Yes, I meant to say "script" because having one is the most efficient way to stay out of trouble with interpersonal communication around difficult subjects. Similar to how lawyers talk their clients through a court appearance, I rehearse with my clients how we think the conversation will go. We adjust the script to fit our vision of the desired outcome. If you have crafted an answer to every question or rejection someone might throw your way, you can avoid becoming confused or overwhelmed and sabotaging the outcome.

If you have access to hypnosis or any form of therapy that can help you remain centered during challenging events, this is the time to double down on it. The best way to have a positive conversation is to be prepared for the worst kind of argument. I have all my clients listen to two visualizations the week prior to having the conversation. First thing in the morning, they listen to a short visualization called "New Beginnings," where we focus on all the greatness that will come after the divorce is complete. Just as athletes do with their visualizations, I get my clients feeling the accomplishment before it has happened so it can begin to form as a reality. The clearer you can see it, the easier it will be to make it real. The other visualization is for right before they go to sleep and focuses on preparing the nervous system to remain relaxed while having difficult conversations. It is subconscious programming used to override our natural flight/freeze/fight response and help us remain calm no matter what happens. How you react if conversations intensify will come down to applying learned ways to bring yourself back to center when everything is spiraling out of control.

TELLING THE KIDS

There are different schools of thought around how you should tell your children you are ending your marriage. When should it happen? Should you sit all your children down together or do it separately? I like to find out from my clients what the family dynamics are, if there are power structures that need to be respected, and what their intuition tells them. From there, I will make my suggestions. However, in general, I tend to prefer talking to the children before friends and family because it makes them feel prioritized. I also suggest you are open to the possibility that this conversation, far from being a devastating event, can be a deep bonding moment with your children. We are so caught up in creating terrible scenarios in our heads that we ignore the reality that our children might be well aware of the impending separation, be OK with it, or as often happens, are happy for a change so the hostile environment can end. Be willing to receive with grace whatever reaction your children have and to detach from any expected outcomes.

If you have teenagers, I suggest you talk to them separately from their younger siblings, especially if the gap in maturity or age is noticeable. The older kids' reactions tend to dictate how the younger siblings react, so it is important you have the conversation separately if you think this will be the case. It also gives them a sense of importance, and they might become your allies simply out of appreciation for your desire to treat them as an adult.

No matter what your situation, use the same steps outlined for the conversation with your spouse on Stage 3. The parts specific to this conversation are:

- Do it together. It is crucial for your kids to feel safe with the uncertainty ahead, and seeing you and your spouse as a united front will be greatly reassuring. They may not be as worried, and they may perceive that this collaboration implies you are going to try your best to avoid conflict.

- When having the conversation with your spouse, analyzing the reasons behind the need for divorce tends to be counter-productive and might escalate to conflict. It is different with children. Often, they are not aware of what has happened for the marriage to disintegrate, and their confusion will not allow them to listen to what you have to tell them. Find a reason they can understand, and share that with them. For example: "We do not love each other as spouses or best friends any-more," "We want to do different things," or "We want to see or be with other people." Be honest, but do not overexpose them to details they do not need to know. Do not go into blaming the other person or becoming argumentative—this will only make them feel like they have to take sides.

- Let them know you will do your best to ensure their life is not turned upside down. There will be changes, but you will try to keep them to a minimum, and although you will not be mar-ried, you will always be a family. Tell them how things are go-ing to work. If you have already discussed a co-parenting plan, share it with them. Talk about housing arrangements, what will change, and what will not.

- Ask them if they understand or need clarification, some time to process, or if they have anything to share. If they have any questions, answer them honestly. If you do not know the an-swer, tell them you do not know but you are working together to figure it out. If you are not working together, don't lie—just tell them you do not know but will let them know soon.

- Reassure them that they can always talk to you, your spouse, or whoever they feel comfortable with (friends, relatives, or therapists). Let them know you will not be offended or hurt if they need to process the divorce with someone else. Don't bring in therapy or professional help just yet; let all this sink in, then assess as time goes by. But please do not ignore the possibility that they might need extra help, and if they ask for it, make sure they know you will do your best to provide it.

TELLING RELATIVES
AND FRIENDS

You might be surprised to know a lot of my clients are far more terrified of telling their parents, siblings, or friends about the divorce than they are their spouse or children. Anxiety arises from fear of judgment, criticism, shaming, and ultimately, conflict. They are also scared of losing those who decide they have to take sides. These fears are perfectly justifiable, but with the right communication techniques, you may control the narrative and enlist them as your allies instead of suffering their lack of support.

We utilize the same approach described for the conversation with your spouse and will also focus on the following points:

- Have empathy for their point of view: Older relatives and people from a previous generation don't understand how you can go against something they were indoctrinated to preserve at all costs. Often, they resent the fact they couldn't do it themselves and are jealous of what they perceive as unfair because they did not have access to it. Ultimately, they tend to project on us their ideas and beliefs around divorce, which tend to be antiquated and out of touch with our current reality. Be willing to listen to them if you have the emotional capacity, and if you do not, set boundaries and explain how they can support you.

- Work with a divorce coach, therapist, or an appropriate mindfulness teacher to not be afraid of judgment, criticism, and loved ones' attempts to persuade you into staying. All of this is to be expected from some family dynamics. It does not mean it is justified, but if you expect it and learn ways to defuse the intensity of their approach, you will remain in control.

- Understand that they might be worried about your future. Unless you are in an abusive relationship, they might not see how divorce would be a change for the better. They worry about the financial and emotional challenges they perceive you will endure. With the help of a professional coach, you can learn to develop an impenetrable confidence to know what is best for you.

- No matter how friends and relatives react initially, the majority will most likely end up supporting you unconditionally, offering the shoulders you need to cry on, or even helping you financially. Instead of focusing on everything that can go wrong, visualize all the ways it can go right.

- Set boundaries within the first conversation to lead the way for the rest of the process. Some people assume we want to hear what a horrible human our soon-to-be ex is; yet you might want the opposite so you will not slide into hatred before negotiations. Learn the ways you can ask for it without sounding too defensive or making them feel offended. There is no clause in the divorce agreement that says how relationships with friends and relatives will evolve. It is up to you to set those parameters with well-constructed conversations.

- Make it clear that this is happening, and if you do not feel like explaining the reasons, then don't. Communicate that the time to analyze the marriage is over. Be assertive in letting them know this is the beginning of a new arrangement, and you would love their support and encouragement moving forward, not "How to Fix Your Marriage" advice.

- Ask for what you need from them: support, no criticism, no judgment, financial assistance, childcare, and whatever else you might require during this transition. Often, others want to help, but we need to tell them clearly what that entails and not expect them to just know, especially if they have not gone through divorce themselves.

- Whatever happens, do not take it personally. More often than not, friends and relatives are probably doing the best to love you, but it's easy to misconstrue their efforts as personal attacks. Having said that, if they are reacting in ways that promote fear and anxiety and do not kindly receive your feedback to stop those behaviors, consider putting distance between you and them to preserve your sanity. You have permission to not let them hijack your divorce and project guilt or shame onto you.

STAGE 7:
The Logistics Of Divorce

It might be shocking for some that this is the last stage of the divorce process. One of the reasons we have divorced so incorrectly in the past is because we have put the cart before the horse. We have tried to do the logistics before we dealt with the emotions. This is a recipe for endless strife and long, difficult negotiations that might end with your case going to court.

If you have created your Divorce Team as suggested on Stage 5, you have a winning chance at an inexpensive and fast divorce that will not leave you with emotional baggage. Work with each professional to reach agreements so you can avoid making financial and emotional mistakes. A few more pointers I provide to all my clients include the following:

- Become financially literate: Even if your spouse has been the breadwinner and/or the one who has always handled the financial decisions, now is your time to step up and learn financial mastery. If you are working with a financial advisor, they may teach you the basics on how to keep a hold on your finances. If you are feeling overwhelmed about having to learn this for the first time, you can shift from an "I have to" mentality to "I get to." You get to take control over your financial future and bet on yourself becoming more successful than you ever were during your marriage. The other advantage of being financially literate is that it helps you create a financial plan for post-divorce life that takes all income and expenses into consideration for your new living arrangements. You will not have unwanted surprises if you can anticipate and budget for your new lifestyle.

- Remove the emotional attachment to assets: This is especially complicated to achieve on your own, but with professional help, you can work through the emotional triggers to material possessions. The most challenging one is the family home because we mistakenly associate it with family stability. Many initially feel victorious because they kept ownership of the family home, only to end up drowning trying to make payments on one income and with no possibility to refinance. I present my clients with the real cost of keeping the family home, and if they are not able to afford it, they avoid a colossal mistake and gain something else during negotiations. The more logical and emotionally detached you are about splitting assets, the easier negotiations will flow, and the higher your chance to remain financially strong post-divorce.

- Understand that a custody plan is for your children's benefit, not exclusively your own: Another remarkably strong attachment that is hard to navigate on our own is full access to the children. It is extremely difficult to consider that unless you are aiming for full custody, you will not see your kids every day. I understand that the incomprehensible agony of spending days away from them may be too much to bear, but I am a firm proponent that children need access to both parents. Unless their safety is compromised in the presence of one parent alone, consider the disadvantaged position for your children if they lose access to one parent because the other would not allow it. Furthermore, although it can be hard to believe at first, you may grow to appreciate the time you get for yourself. Many of my clients get to travel, learn new hobbies, and even build übersuccessful businesses with the time they now devote to themselves without the constraints of full-time parenting.

- Tie all loose ends: Once you sign the divorce decree and it is finalized by the system, take some time to celebrate. You did something huge, and hopefully, you did not just "go through it" but managed to "grow through it." I bet it was extremely painful at times, and yet you survived, and with the right professional help, probably thrived. After celebrating this major win, it is time to tie up all the loose ends, so you do not have to deal with issues later on. This includes but is not limited to the following:

- Restructuring the debt and deed for the family home and other previously jointly held property/ventures

- Closing joint bank accounts and credit cards

- Getting a credit report to ensure you do not have any lingering debt or future liabilities under both names (unless you agreed to them)

- Finding insurance options in case there is failure to pay child support or alimony, so you can act rapidly

- Notifying schools and other relevant kids' environments of the changes and how communication should be handled moving forward

Finally, you should continue working with your transition and divorce coach to start your new life with the emotional resources you need.

10-STEP PROCESS
FOR HEALING

Having a Holistic Divorce is an art that cannot be simplified in a few pages, but what follows is an overview of the process, so you have a frame of reference if you wish to create your own. Remember, this is not a linear timeline. I have organized the steps by level of priority to make your process easier, but I am not implying that you work on acceptance once and be done with it. Each step will have to be readdressed during the process, and even after the divorce is complete. It is my hope that you learn each of the steps during your divorce, then continue applying them to all areas of your life. I wish I had mastered conscious communication during my first marriage, but diving into it for my divorce granted me the skills to have productive conversations with my second husband and avoid the classic pitfalls of messy communication.

STEP 1–
ACCEPTANCE

One of the most disturbing forces at play during divorce is resistance—we simply do not want to admit what is happening. It doesn't matter if you or your partner are the one initiating divorce; you can expect an avoidance to change and resistance to feeling the emotions of divorce. You might feel like you are losing your comfort, security, and even sanity. At times, the pain and grief for what is being lost might feel unbearable and as if nothing will be normal again. If this sounds familiar or you can relate in any way, welcome to the club! There is absolutely nothing wrong with you. It is all part of the process, and you will be OK. You may feel tempted to keep busy and avoid feeling these emotions, but if you want to heal, the key is to first *accept them* so you can move on to the next stage—processing them. Let me elaborate on the completely normal emotional responses to divorce you will likely experience, so you know you are not alone or going crazy:

- Desire to numb feelings—you may find yourself wanting to diminish the physical and emotional discomfort by triggering all your coping mechanisms. While it might seem like you're making wrong decisions and creating destructive habits, it may simply be your mind's way of protecting you from feeling overwhelming emotions.

- Disrupted sleep patterns—not being able to sleep or sleeping too much is completely normal. Our "worrying gene" tends to get activated as soon as we tuck into bed. Learn techniques to put that monkey mind to rest, so you can get the restoration time you need and avoid the use of sleeping pills.

- Changing eating habits—it's normal to have either almost no appetite at all or a need to eat nonstop. Our culture has a complicated relationship with food that goes beyond its purpose as nourishment. In times of crisis, we gravitate toward food that might not be the healthiest choice in a search of comfort. Or conversely, we might avoid eating altogether as a form of self-punishment. Try and adhere to healthy choices, but please do not be hard on yourself. This is a phase, and it will pass. Do not add more judgment and criticism to your already overwhelmed nervous system by stressing about your eating habits, which will likely be normalized when the process is over.

- Roller coaster of emotional energy with extreme ups and downs—as a direct result of the emotional highs and lows, you may feel emotionally and physically drained, and this will be taxing to your body and relationships. It's important to let others know you are going through a complicated change and need their patience when you are acting out of character.

- Depression—there is so much uncertainty about the future that we tend to imagine all the worst-case scenarios, which can leave us feeling hopeless. Even people leaving abusive relationships will initially hit depressive states before they can rejoice in their new path. Fear of the unknown is *that* ingrained into our system.

- Desolation and desperation—lack of hope and faith that the future will be brighter is a prevailing emotion as we wonder if we will ever find love again, if our children will suffer, or if our financial future will be impaired. Please be gentle and compassionate with yourself when you are feeling hopelessly lost. You are going through a lot, and you are doing the best you can.

- Reduced concentration and lack of focus—the anxiety of not knowing how it is all going to end can use so much energy that you might find it hard to focus. If at all possible, take some time away from work and household responsibilities to dive into the Inner Work so you can remove some of the worry and anxiety.

- Feeling isolated—even those with a strong support system can feel not fully understood. Friends' advice might conflict with your needs. The problem is that best intentions do not translate into best advice. Unless they have experienced what you are going through and achieved what you are aiming for, their advice is not relevant and can make you feel lonely.

- Feeling uncontrollable anger or rage—this is especially possible if you are identifying as the victim and feeling as if you have been wronged. It is important to learn how to move from a space of anger and betrayal to one of calm and trust by exiting the victim mentality.

- Experiencing dramatic mood changes and lack of control—you will feel low for the first weeks or months of your divorce process. After that, you'll start to feel more like your old self. You'll start to rationalize things, and you'll begin to work out what to do next. This is a turning point. Now you are thinking about your future and ready to move on. The pain will still be there, but you will be ready to find the tools to work through the pain and create the next chapter of your life.

STEP 2–

FEELING ALL THE EMOTIONS

Let's start this step by highlighting an important point: your feelings, no matter how much you dislike them, are absolutely valid, even if those around you unconsciously judge or shame you for having them. Friends might say, "You should not feel this way about (fill in the blank)," but that is their own projection of how they feel about divorce, and that has no purpose in your healing process. *Feelings are not to be judged; they just need to be felt.* This may seem like an overly simple statement, but it is not an easy task unless we have been taught how to do it.

Every emotion we consider negative has a way of getting amplified the more we try to silence it. Emotions ask to be faced so they can release their energetic hold on us. The visualization and journaling exercises I create for my clients are designed to help move them through each emotion, find the boundary or ending of the feeling, and release it, allowing them to shift onto the next emotional layer. There is a scale of emotions and a natural completion for each one, but you move to a higher vibrational emotion only when you have truly experienced and acknowledged the preceding emotion fully. Resist your emotions by numbing or self-destructive coping mechanisms, and you are simply postponing the healing cycle.

So how do you feel your feelings? You sit with them. Like the poet Rumi says, invite them to tea, be grateful for the messages they bring, as they have been sent to guide you. While you are sitting with your feelings, observe them. What is the story I keep telling when I'm feeling anxious? Where in my body do I feel it? Is there a memory attached to that feeling? Do not try to fix your emotions or turn them into a pleasant feeling. Be comfortable in the discomfort and locate where the emotional charge originates. You can almost always trace it back to something from your past that is creating fear in the present moment.

If instead of sitting with your feelings—observing them and letting them pass—you allow your ego to step in, your mind may spiral out of control with all the horrible scenarios that can be created from a place of fear. Your ego is trying to keep you safe and will discourage you from engaging in anything that causes upheaval in your life. But suppression can make anxiety escalate into depression and hopelessness, allowing the vicious cycle to continue and trauma to settle in your body and mind for the long run.

The three most relevant human basic needs to be seen, heard, and understood, correlate directly to the three big emotions of divorce that manifest into expressions of anger: sadness at not feeling heard, shame from not feeling seen, and guilt from feeling unworthy of love. Fear of these needs not being met, during and post-divorce, is the precursor to many unnecessary legal battles, which may be prevented if those emotions are properly managed. No matter how overpowering, all emotions lose their intensity when we are willing to look closer for the hidden messages behind them, understand they are part of the divorce journey, and give ourselves permission to process them. Let's pull back the curtain and take a peek into the Emotions of Divorce.

ANGER

The energy of anger touches all of us. Some have a direct and quick connection to it; for others, it simmers to a critical point, then it must be expressed, often in unhealthy ways. We have to be conscious of how we choose to release this powerful emotion because it can make or break our ability to navigate divorce to a successful completion. I call anger "The Arrow with No Target." Although it might be hard to believe, anger is not caused by someone or something outside of us. Anger lives in our body, buried deep in the tissues and organs as trauma from the past that we did not get a chance to emotionally digest. It is an arrow—or a basket of arrows, depending on how much anger you have stored in your lifetime— and it is constantly looking for a target to hit. It is uncomfortable to admit we get satisfaction from shooting that arrow in the direction of someone who has violated our beliefs. It is even more disturbing to recognize that we get immediate relief from the pain we are carrying when the people we target are hit so efficiently that they become hurt too.

As conscious humans, we do not want to admit any of this is true. Instead, we either rage against the other person for their transgression, or we simply repress our anger. Yet anger is not an energy that dissipates when it is suppressed or unleashed—it either remains in the subconscious, forcing us into harmful decisions, or creates damaging scenarios in real life. Rather than lashing out or repressing anger, I encourage my clients to sit with their anger and search for the hidden message it holds. Once the message is understood, the messenger (anger) can leave the stage, and you have a chance to peacefully overcome the trigger without regrettable consequences.

Although I am aware it is easier said than done, the first step is to feel the anger without judgment. Do not think there is anything wrong with feeling rage inside of you. Do not try to suppress it because you want to be "nice." As long as we take ownership of our anger—meaning we feel and accept it—we have a chance to avoid the destructive consequences of projecting it onto others. When you get angry during your divorce, ask yourself, "What is really making me angry? Is it the situation itself, or the story I created based on a perception from past events?" Can you see the madness in it? Reality is not what we see; it is what we perceive it to be.

The next time you feel anger rising up, stop to breathe, recognize its presence, and take time alone to listen attentively for its hidden clues. Most conflict can be prevented if we take the time to feel the frustration and release it before interacting with anyone else. If you are with someone, ask for space to process by saying, "I can't talk about this right now," or "Please let me think about it and I will get back to you." If the person who is "causing" the anger reacts by attacking you and will not listen to your request, walk away. Let them know you will not participate in this interaction, but you will be ready to address the issue again after you have a chance to sit with it and cool down. When we allow ourselves to enter into confrontation, both parties have already lost the battle. It becomes hard to reach agreements and resolutions when instead of communicating, our angry egos are battling until further damage is done.

Often, sitting with anger is simply too uncomfortable. You can help your body calm down by engaging in activities to release the emotional charge. I am not referring to meditation or any other calming strategy that does not involve movement; the opposite is needed when anger is in your system. Anything to change the chemistry in your body from stress hormone overload to dopamine release can be more beneficial: running, working out, dancing, screaming into a pillow, punching a kicking bag, or even a fast-paced walk.

Once you have taken the time to connect to your anger and release it through physical activities, you can then use conscious communication to express to others why you are feeling angry and what can be done to process it. Communicating anger is very different from expressing anger, and it does not equate to becoming violent, abusive, or aggressive. Exhibiting such behavior is the opposite of owning your anger—that is anger owning you. Relying on the principles of conscious communication will help you shift from trying to aim the arrow straight for someone's heart to putting it down and negotiating to de-escalate conflict.

GRIEF

If you are a visual person like me, you might enjoy the image I associate with grief. Grief is the emotion I call "The Changing Tides of the Soul." My son gave me the inspiration for the name when I watched him go from having the time of his life building castles on the shoreline to absolute devastation when the Pacific Ocean wiped his hard work away with one sweeping wave. He was inconsolable, and I could not blame him. He felt this terrible loss was unexpected and unfair. Even though he knew tides change rapidly, and I promised him we would build a better castle together, his sadness was stronger than any logic, and he proceeded to sob uncontrollably until grief had run its course and left his body.

This is a magic that children possess and that adults have lost. Children let feelings run their course because they intuit that emotion equals energy in motion, and any attempt to disrupt or suppress it will allow it to live in the subconscious mind and body rather than dissipate. They know we need to face the emotion of grief head-on rather than trying to push it away or put on a smiley face and pretend it is not part of our experience. Grief has to be part of the divorce process because you are losing an important part of your life.

The dreams and future you thought you would have are disappearing along with your marriage.

Try giving sadness space to exist temporarily during this transition without fearing it will become the most prevalent emotion in your life. We are terrified to explore sadness, presuming that if we indulge those feelings, we may head into a deep depression from which we will not be able to escape. If you feel that way, reach out for professional help to navigate this ocean of sadness without drowning in it. Please do not entrust your friends or relatives with this process as they are not trained to handle the nuances of grief and will most likely not be able to sit in your pain while you process it. They will probably encourage you to get it together, get back on the horse, or do whatever else they think it takes to (most likely unsuccessfully) fully release the grief.

With professional guidance, you may find the safety to allow yourself to go down the rabbit hole of emotions and process them in a protected environment. You will most likely feel overwhelmed, and as the first wave of sadness hits, crying will be the main way you allow sadness to pass through you. Go there and spend time feeling and releasing. It will be terribly uncomfortable, but do not halt the process because of the mistaken societal belief that crying is a weakness. It is a way of removing the stored energies from traumatic events so they do not condition the decisions you make about your future. During my divorce, there were weeks when I did not stop crying; but with every tear I shed, I felt years of pain and trauma washing away. You will feel lighter afterward, and your willingness to honor the grieving process as part of healing the trauma of divorce will grant you permission to cry and release as needed. Trust me: your future self will thank you for not carrying this suffering for years.

SHAME AND GUILT

I have not come up with a poetic description for this emotion because in my opinion, it is an artificial one that I hope we will eradicate as a collective unity in the near future. Shame is a peculiar emotion that is not intrinsic to our biological nature. We are indoctrinated into what constitutes shameful behaviors by the society in which we live. It is not an inherent emotion; instead, we are taught to be ashamed with statements such as "Shame on you" or "You should be ashamed of yourself." No child experiences shame unless he has been conditioned to believe his behavior is embarrassing. A child can be angry, sad, tired, or frustrated without needing a grown-up to show them how to feel that way, but they do not know what shame is or how it feels until we teach them. Body shame is the perfect example: a child perceives nothing is wrong with their body until we tell them what we consider perfect bodies to be and how anything different from that standard should make us feel ashamed.

Shame and guilt can get muddled together, but they are different emotions, as you can probably tell simply by the somatic response they create in the body. Shame is a nerve-wracking, heart-pumping, red-faced, "want the earth to swallow me" kind of bodily reaction. Guilt, on the other hand, is a more debilitating corroding of self-worth, as the body feels apathetic, depressed, and lethargic with the heavy weight of intrinsic wrongdoing. Our subconscious language translates those somatic experiences with the programing from shame—*The world hates me because I did something wrong*—and guilt, *I hate myself because I did something wrong*. Perhaps these two statements give us a clue as to why most people in our culture suffer from the mistaken assumption of "there is something wrong with me" and the consequent lack of self-love.

Divorce has been deemed an undesirable aberration to the norm we are expected to obey; we are explicitly told to remain married until death do us part. Anything else is wrong and a failure. Even though divorce is becoming more socially acceptable, in part because of the rapidly growing statistics questioning whether it is an aberration or natural evolution, there is still a stigma and judgment around divorce that becomes internalized as shame and guilt. I cannot stress enough the highly negative impact these disempowering emotions create. Most of my clients who battle suicidal ideation grade their shame and/or guilt as the emotion they feel and struggle with the most.

I utilize the same strategy for shame and guilt as described with previous emotions—instead of suppressing them, I encourage you to observe them and analyze what beliefs are attached to them. However, unlike anger and sadness, shame does not need to be accepted; it needs to be replaced. We have to choose an internal response to counteract the belief that caused shame with an empowering one. Once you accomplish this, you have dismantled any power shame or guilt have as control mechanisms.

Do the Inner Work to release shame around divorce so no societal programming will make you believe you have done anything wrong or failed. Find inspiration from those preaching that the choice to leave a marriage is just as valid as the choice to stay. You have to silence the negative influence from society by listening to a different voice, which you can do easily through social media and professional services. Find teachers, books, and other positive role models for separations or divorces that inspire you, and do not hesitate to harness the power of coaching to help you release shame and guilt.

FEAR

Let's talk about the mother of all the Emotions of Divorce, which actually runs underneath all the previous emotions. Being terrified of making mistakes—or FOFU, fear of fucking up—is the one variable all my clients have in common, and justifiably so. Ignorance is always costly, but even more so during divorce. We are not just talking financially, but emotionally and spiritually too. Not to mention how complicated it is to appeal or reverse decisions already agreed upon and recorded by the court system. But while your fear may be valid, you are still capable of managing it or completely eradicating it from the divorce process.

I call fear "The Straight Jacket for the Sane Ones" as it is usually felt as a maddening, paralyzing force that is responsible for getting us stuck and overwhelmed without fully grasping why. It makes us act in irrational ways that we do not recognize as part of our persona, and if left unchecked, fear might find a cozy place within our psyche and stay with us for the long haul. Fear lights up the same neuropathways engaged in addictive behaviors, which may lead us to believe we can get hooked on the emotion of fear.

The best way to slay the fear dragons of the mind is to shine light on them and watch them dissolve. Courage is the antidote to fear, and it can only be accessed by feeling the fear and doing whatever scares you anyway. I have clients who score fear as their most prevalent emotion participate in a "Fear Fantasizing" exercise. I ask them to list all their biggest fears, being as specific as possible. We then create a fantasy (or you might say "nightmare") where all these fears come true. We sit with that "rock bottom" scenario, then create their very own "comeback story" by figuring out the strategies that would counteract the damage done. It might seem like a masochist's approach to dealing with fear, but fear cannot exist in hope, and hope is the result of knowing you have options. Once you truly understand that, you will be OK no matter how bad things get because fear loses most of its power. The way to completely remove fear from the divorce process and avoid self-sabotage is to keep facing it. Every time you feel fear creep in, sit with it, and listen to what your subconscious is telling you about what scares you. Remember, the only way out is through.

STEP 3
DROP MISTAKEN BELIEFS

For decades, society believed the human body was not physically able to run a mile in less than four minutes. In the 1940s, the mile record was 4:01, and no matter how hard runners of all races, nationalities, and backgrounds tried, it was impossible to push it any lower. On May 6, 1954, Roger Bannister broke the four-minute barrier by getting it done in 3:59. As puzzled as everybody was by this remarkable feat, they attributed his success to great training and an extraordinary ability. They also concluded the performance would be impossible for another human to repeat. Barely a year after Bannister broke the record, another runner hit the same time, then another, and so on, until it was universally acknowledged that hitting this time was doable. Once the world witnessed one human achieving the feat, there was no excuse not to replicate it. The same can happen with how we view divorce. With enough people—my clients and me included—proving it can be done without the drama and trauma, it is my hope we can inspire others to end relationships and marriages that are no longer part of the life they want for themselves.

Tim Ferriss redefined the established American nine-to-five

grind through his remarkable book *The 4-Hour Workweek*, and he said, "Most people fail not because they lack the skills or aptitude to reach their goal but because they simply do not believe they can reach it." I cannot stress how important it is for the success of your low-conflict divorce that you believe it can be done. Let me elaborate on the most prevalent disempowering beliefs and how we can reframe them to cultivate a mindset where a civilized divorce is possible.

THE BELIEF OF "THE BROKEN HOME"

It makes me shudder when kids from divorced families are immediately labeled as kids from broken homes. The general, although unproven, correlation between divorce and a disrupted family environment needs to be removed as it has no grounds and merely adds to the stress parents face. There are plenty of kids who are seriously impaired by living in married households where the level of mental and even physical abuse from unhappy spouses is unbearable. Yet these are considered stable homes, and they are not as badly judged as divorced households, simply because the parents are still married. This is insanity!

What is truly devastating to children is not divorce but perpetuating an environment of chronic dissatisfaction and unresolved conflict. If we sacrifice our fulfillment in the relationship for the sake of the children, they will view our misery as an acceptable standard for love in their own lives. If they are witnessing anger, resentment, and disrespect, their subconscious minds will classify that as the way people love. This is the real danger—not a "broken home" but kids trying to make sense of how turmoil is considered love and using that model as the blueprint for future relationships.

THE BELIEF OF
"STAYING TOGETHER FOR THE KIDS"

Although a well-intentioned reason to preserve the union, the reality is that in many cases, there is no guarantee this decision will benefit anyone. I lived in a household where my parents' preferred way of communication was yelling and verbal fights. Although their marriage was shattered with no way to reconcile, they decided to "stay together for the children," and we lived for almost a decade in an environment of hostility, frustration, and bitterness until my father finally moved out. My siblings and I felt nothing but relief when the day arrived that we did not have to endure their suffering in our lives on a daily basis. The Holistic Divorce paradigm encourages people to instead say, "We are separating *for* the children." When we understand how our kids feed off our emotional states, we will strive to offer them only a positive environment, within or outside a marital union.

I divorced "for my children" so they would have a chance to live in a nourishing and positive environment, even if it was with one parent at a time. My ex and I did not fight in front of the children, and we were extremely respectful toward each other, but I did not want my kids to grow up believing that our friendly but distant relationship was all love can offer. There is also an emerging trend of children benefitting greatly from having a broader extended family with different but equally loving parenting role models. You can also use this opportunity as a chance to explain how everything in life is impermanent and that change can be welcomed. The art of navigating change and transitions is a much more valuable skill than the "grin and bear it" approach.

THE BELIEF OF
"MY SPOUSE DID NOTHING WRONG;
HE/SHE DOES NOT DESERVE THIS"

Our culture has a stronghold on the unforgiving message that divorce is devastating for the spouses, the children, and even your friends and relatives, but the truth is, *you get to choose how to frame your divorce.* There is a tendency to look for someone to blame, but if we understand that divorce can be a positive transformation for everybody involved, there is no reason for finger-pointing. We can't blame anyone for wanting to grow at a different pace or chase different dreams, or for simply not being able to love us the way we need to be loved. Even in instances where unspeakable transgressions were made, adhering to victimhood will deter the ability to heal, and I suggest you choose differently.

Release these limitations, and accept that you and your ex do not need an extenuating circumstance to want out. In the past, we needed a reason to divorce. We had to prove a spouse failed at delivering on his/her obligations or that the union had become unbearable. Today, you can have a "no-fault" divorce, and there is a growing number of marriages ending without the need for any kind of negative justification behind the decision. Do not play the blame game on you or your partner; otherwise, you risk creating more anger, resentment, and feelings of inadequacy that will poison the process and add unnecessary drama.

THE BELIEF OF
"THE FAILED MARRIAGE"

Can we please add a new narrative in which we accept that just because a relationship has reached its conclusion, it does not necessarily mean it was a failure? I find it bizarre how society has indoc-trinated us to believe that a long-lasting relationship is the only type of successful relationship. *Longevity should not be the defining factor when evaluating the success of a relationship.* We can also accept that in today's society, marriage is an environment for both partners to grow and thrive in, not something to tolerate at all costs—even when riddled in misery and stagnation—as our previous generations did, to avoid the stigma of the "Failed Marriage."

I consider my marriage of sixteen years a resounding success. We built an empire of businesses and financial abundance, created two incredible humans who are balanced and kind, and shared a beauti-ful love story until the end. When facing the truth that your partner-ship has expired, you can aim for a resolution where everybody wins and you retain the lessons learned along the way, or you can stay in hatred, and fight to undo all the positives your relationship brought. You get to choose whether you failed or learned.

THE BELIEF OF
THE "PERPETRATOR VS. VICTIM"

We mistakenly presume that the person who asks for the divorce also *wants* the divorce, whereas in the majority of cases, this could not be further from the truth. Statistically, women initiate 70 per-cent of divorces. They tend to be the ones starting the process, not because they are creating a problem, but because they want to find a solution to a problem that already exists: their relationship has ended, and they wish to cancel the contract attached to it. Does that make them the perpetrator? Does it mean they want to end the relationship? That they are ready and willing to divorce? Are they supposed to bear the judgment and criticism of divorce because they started the process? Do we automatically presume their spouse is the victim and should be showered with support while they are punished?

We live in a peculiar paradigm where we have been programmed to believe that we need to be madly in love in order to tie the knot, but at the same time, if that love disappears, we think it is totally fine to stay in a loveless marriage. The message is: if you can put up with your partner—including when communication is derogatory or offensive—then you should stay in the marriage. Unless he or she abuses you or fails to contribute financially to the family unit, do not ask for a divorce. The issue arises when you realize you want way more than the status quo. When you feel you deserve better and can no longer be satisfied by what society deems as acceptable standards, you will no longer settle for mediocre or even good enough. You will want greatness, and I admire you for that and hope society as a whole will offer the same respect. My question to those who insist on criticizing your courage and want to turn you into the perpetrator is: what is wrong about having dreams and ambitions that cannot be realized within the marriage? In my opinion, absolutely nothing. Let's stop labeling anyone as a victim or perpetrator and instead offer the support they need.

STEP 4—
FORGIVENESS AND LETTING GO ON REPEAT

Author Alan Cohen once said, "You can change the past when you change the way you see it." In order to move forward, we need to let go of anything holding us back. Often, we hold on because we are afraid of what we may lose when we let go. We associate letting go with having less, when the reality is that we are creating space for bigger and better things to enter our life. Once you master the art of letting go of what you thought were mistakes, you are ready to begin the forgiveness process. What others call mistakes, I call learning—to me, FAIL stands for First Attempt In Learning. There is no need to add disappointment and all the other negative emotions to what are nothing more than steps in the learning process. Reframe every mistake as a lesson so you can forgive yourself, leave the past behind, and create the future you truly crave.

Whole libraries have been written about the subject of forgiveness, and nearly all religions and spiritual schools claim that to free your soul of suffering, you must become a master of forgiveness. During divorce, there is an unconscious fear of releasing old pain and letting go of the anger toward your spouse because we are wired to resist change, even if it is for the better. But nothing will change until *we* change, and forgiveness is the path to ending resentment and letting go of *our* suffering, not theirs.

Forgiveness is not excusing wrongful actions. It does not mean we are condoning any unacceptable behavior, and it certainly does not imply consent for future actions. It is a release designed for you to feel lighter moving forward because you are not carrying negative emotions any further. Cultivate a mindset where outside circumstances do not affect your emotions, and be prepared to forgive the actions of others. Forgiveness is not an intellectual process but an embodiment one—you cannot rationalize your path into forgiveness. We consciously set the intention to forgive someone, then work on embedding that decision into our subconscious by daily thoughts and actions. Your subconscious has to be on the same forgiveness program as your conscious intention. I teach my clients to engage their subconscious using a forgiveness ritual from an ancient Hawaiian practice called ho'oponopono. It is part of the embodiment of forgiveness, and the result is genuine closure that heals all wounds.

How do you heal yourself with ho'oponopono? By recognizing that whatever comes to you is your creation—the outcome of unresolved memories buried in your mind—then taking responsibility for whatever errors of body, speech, and mind were caused by those unprocessed traumas and requesting Divine Intelligence within yourself to release your guilt. The Hawaiian concept of kuleana is rooted in the idea that you are responsible for the good, the bad, and the ugly in your life. The world you create and live in is your masterpiece or your hell. But do not confuse responsibility with fault. Kuleana simply means you are responsible for fixing yourself in order to fix whatever or whoever seems to be the origin of your problem. It empowers you to be the creator of your reality, which is the best mindset to have when starting your next great chapter.

THE HO'OPONOPONO RITUAL:

I have created a ritual similar to the ho'oponopono ancient practice Hawaiians used to resolve conflict in their communities and achieve forgiveness. You will need

- four sheets of paper and a pen;

- sage or palo santo; and

- any other special healing items you love (i.e., rose quartz crystal, music or mantras that soothe your soul, teas, Epsom salts).

STEP 1: SET THE STAGE

- Choose a time when you will not be disturbed for an hour.

- Set up a calming, peaceful environment; maybe even take an Epsom salt bath with calming essential oils.

- Create a beautiful altar with flowers, pictures of your loved ones, crystals, or any other grounding props.

- Make some tea to help you relax.

- Play some high-vibrational music (classic piano or any playlist with mantras).

- Get your mind into a neutral space with a five-minute meditation focused on your breathing—slow inhale and exhale.

STEP 2: PROCESS

Time to get honest and let feelings be expressed. You will write a letter on four sheets of paper, addressed to your ex-partner (or soon-to-be-ex-partner). Write on top of one page: I Love You. On the second sheet: I Am Sorry. The third: Please Forgive Me. The last one: Thank You.

On the I Love You sheet: Write down the reasons why you loved your ex. Even if all you can feel is resentment and anger now, there was a time when you deeply loved that person. Go back to that time and write down all the things you used to love about them. Start with all the ways they made you feel special and loved, or how they relate to you or your children. I know this might be hard, but nobody said forgiveness is easy.

For the I am Sorry sheet: Write down all the things for which you are sorry. This can include things you did or said, things you did not say or do, what you think were mistakes, and all the ways in which you hurt your ex. This one is especially hard if you feel like they have treated you badly, have done unreasonable things, or said horrible insults, but this is about finding the moments *you* dropped the ball.

For the Please Forgive Me sheet: Ask from the bottom of your heart for their forgiveness for all the ways you might have failed them, for not being able to stay together, and for whatever it is that might be causing resentment. Accept responsibility for your part in the divorce, even if you feel like you're the victim and did nothing wrong, and try and accept the fact there was a time when you did not fulfill their expectations either.

For the Thank You sheet: Write down all the things for which you are grateful to your ex from the past and the present, and what you want to be thankful for in the future. Even if all you can write is "I'm thankful for our children" or "I'm thankful you taught me what I do not want," go into detail about anything you can see as a blessing. It is very important you are not sarcastic: no writing "Thank you for ruining Thanksgiving." Instead, find true examples, no matter how small, of acts or words from your ex for which you are genuinely grateful.

You might cry for the entirety of the ritual, and that's OK. Let it happen, and see if once the grief is released, you can shift to a more empathetic view. If you feel rage or any other emotions arise, do not judge; just let it be, and if possible, release it. Cry, scream at a picture of your ex, or punch a pillow if you have to. Allow this part of the process to be a chance to let any suppressed feelings surface so they can be forever gone.

STEP 3: CLEANSE

Now that you have mentally shifted, take extra measures to clear the remains of any negative energies that have come to the surface. Cleanse yourself and your space with palo santo or sage, take an Epsom salt bath, or go for a walk in nature if you can. Every time you feel triggered by your ex, practice ho'oponopono and the powerful forces of Repentance, Forgiveness, Gratitude, and Love, for healing and transmuting suffering. Think of them, and state the following four lines:

I'm sorry.

Please forgive me.

Thank you.

I love you.

Add in any other affirmations to yourself, such as:

I accept the way you choose to behave. I have no control over you or your actions, but I have full control over my reaction to them.

I recognize your actions have no power over me because I am not the victim of your actions.

I am in charge of how I feel and how I perceive this and anything else you have done in the past that might have felt hurtful.

STEP 5–
THE 3 PS: PRACTICE, PATIENCE, AND PERSEVERANCE

I want you to remember the saying: the day you plant the seed is not the day you eat the fruit. During the divorce process, we are put to the test continuously to practice being patient and humble and to show the perseverance to keep moving forward without worrying. When we are in turmoil, we want to move through it as quickly as possible, but divorce does not work that way. You have to slow down to analyze your conscious and subconscious intentions on a daily basis, to process emotions, and to integrate the Inner Work you are engaged in to produce the results you want.

Practice the continuous repetition of new, positive ways to regulate your nervous system so you can act, rather than react, to outside stimuli. As I work with my clients on their triggers, we illuminate ways to counteract those triggers by creating new response patterns. Once you learn this approach, you can apply it to all relationships that tend to throw you into emotional dysregulation and use it to help regain the control you previously gave away. It does not happen overnight, but practice makes progress. You are rewiring your neurological network to have new responses to old triggers, and before you know it, few things will upset you deeply.

Patience is the embodiment of understanding the principle that there is a higher power working in our favor, provided we remain calm and allow it to do its thing. Patience proves our ultimate trust in the process and allows us to resist our human need to meddle with it. We have to learn to experience any setback and delay in our divorce not as an obstacle but as the universe's behind-the-scenes efforts to rearrange the results in our favor. If we get frustrated with any delay or return to the negotiation table, we disrupt the flow of blessings trying to find their way to us. Breath work is a great ally to deploy when patience is running low. I suggest you learn breathing techniques to lower the stress response impatience triggers.

Perseverance is often confused with patience, but in my book, these are two different tools with separate purposes. Patience provides you time and understanding. It helps you release expectations and your tether to desired outcomes, which might be creating the resistance that's keeping them from coming true. Perseverance is the daily recommitment to your dreams and the continuous devotional work needed to manifest them. It is the discipline that strengthens your resolve when obstacles arise so you will not be thrown off balance. Once your divorce is over, you will be able to apply this skill to achieve all the goals you set for your post-divorce life.

STEP 6–
ADOPT POSITIVE PRACTICES, A.K.A. SELF-LOVE

One of the biggest challenges my clients face is taking care of themselves as they are going through the emotional ups and downs of divorce. Some are so overwhelmed by the chaos ahead that they struggle to keep up with nutritional and fitness needs. I am a firm believer that a healthy body leads to a balanced mind, and considering some of the most important decisions of our life occur during the divorce proceedings, creating positive habits is strongly advised. The basic ones I suggest you start practicing are:

1: CREATE AND ENFORCE BOUNDARIES

The skill of creating and enforcing boundaries is rather complex, but a simple way to start is by saying yes to everything that makes you feel joy and no to anything that robs you of peace of mind, including other people's advice and demands. The divorce journey—especially the negotiation part—will be your training ground to practice setting and enforcing healthy boundaries. Sometimes declining by text or email can be less confrontational. You can start there and work your way toward doing it in person without feeling guilty about respecting your own wishes. That is an act of self-love, not selfishness.

2: MEDITATION

I would love to demystify meditation for those who feel they cannot calm their monkey mind and reframe it as awareness: think of meditation as "observation and gratitude time." You might not be able to stop the stream of thoughts, but your objective is simply to observe them without judgment. Just be curious. Set a timer for five minutes, take five deep, slow breaths, and sit with your thoughts. When you are done, reflect on what theme emerged. Were your thoughts centered around fear? Were you hopeful? Was your mind obsessing about past events? Dreaming about the future? You will begin recognizing the patterns you are programmed to repeat, and you will be able to reinforce the positive ones and replace the disempowering ones.

3: CHERISH TIME BY YOURSELF

Some of my most courageous clients went on solo trips to clear their minds from the familiarity that was keeping them stuck in pain and from everybody's influencing opinions. They all report how terrifying it was at the beginning but how they felt unstoppable once they became comfortable outside of their comfort zone. They learned to be self-sufficient and came back feeling stronger and confident they could take on anything. Time alone may give you the courage you are lacking to have the difficult conversations and negotiations with your ex.

4: DO NOT LET MONEY FEARS BLOCK YOU

Although this might sound like a self-promoting plug, I want to make it clear that this next part is not about selling my services. But if you are considering divorce, please, I beg you to consider hiring a divorce coach. I am certain that in the near future, few people will attempt the process without the help of a professionally trained divorce coach. This is not an easy process you can simply DIY, and getting the right qualified help can be the difference between a divorce you are proud of or one you will forever regret.

5: CONNECT TO YOUR INNER VOICE

No matter how convincing other opinions may sound, the truth is that nobody knows what you need better than you do. Sadly, we grow accustomed to looking outside for the answers we carry inside. We have to retrain ourselves to listen to our intuition instead of outsourcing our destiny to other people's advice. Some of my clients report being afraid of listening to their own intuition because they do not trust themselves now that they are facing divorce. They mistakenly believe they have failed and should not be encouraged to make decisions on their own, but I disagree wholeheartedly.

It is my hope by now you understand the fact that your marriage is ending is not an indication you did anything wrong or your innate wisdom misguided you. Maybe you went into the marriage against your intuition's warnings. Perhaps you were meant to live the experiences that relationship created for your spiritual evolution. The right coach or therapist can help you understand how your marriage had a purpose and teach you the skills to quiet the outside voices so you can clearly hear the wisdom of your soul. Listen to what your soul is whispering to you, and follow that truth to make decisions moving forward, even if society does not agree. Remember, sometimes saying goodbye is the most courageous way to say "I love you."

STEP 7–
REWRITE YOUR CONTRACT

When you reach the conclusion that your marriage has ended, you have the potential to start a whole new relationship with your soon-to-be ex based on greater honesty, safer communication, and mutual respect, even if none of these attributes existed before. Once you fully commit to doing the Inner Work for personal growth, you can stop recreating patterns that cause friction in your relationship. When you begin to transform, your relationships will shift as well because others are also invited to show up more authentically, your ex included.

I wish there were more living examples and literature on how to actually accomplish a successful post-divorce relationship. When I was in the thick of rewriting my contract, everybody kept saying, "Darling, what you are trying to do is simply not possible." I temporarily allowed their opinions to become my belief, and I started questioning if it was impossible to end a marriage on the best terms possible and have a civilized relationship post-divorce. Even though every cell in my body said "Yes! It can be done," I did not have any examples to follow. All I could see was that when relationships or marriages ended, there was no new and improved relationship after.

Eventually, I programmed myself to actively choose to forgive the past so I'd have a clean slate from which to work. Journaling was a game changer in this process. Grab your journal and start creating the blueprint for how you want this new contract to be. Give yourself the time and space to dream as big as you want, and keep adding or removing concepts as you advance with your divorce. If you have absolutely no clue as to what is possible, find divorced couples who inspire you and gather ideas from them. Even if they are not in your immediate circle, use books, social media, or any other outlet that showcases how others navigate their divorce and post-divorce bond in a manner that aligns with your goals.

I would not want to end this step without asking you to fill your self-compassion cup to the brim because no matter how much we might want the best relationship with our ex, there can be bumps along the way. I have seen relationships extremely damaged after divorce evolve into civility through the exes healing themselves and persevering in their vision of what they want moving forward. The opposite can also happen, especially as new partners enter the stage. This might be a temporary disconnection, and you might be friendly again when the waters are calm, or your relationship might evolve into a more distant one. Whatever happens, it is OK. Remove the stress around the idea that you have to have the world's best post-divorce relationship—as long as you can be respectful and civilized, you are on the right path.

STEP 8
CONSCIOUS COMMUNICATION

Entire books are written on the art of conscious communication, so I will only present a brief introduction here. If you are serious about learning this most valuable skill, I suggest you either get your hands on the book *Nonviolent Communication* by Marshall Rosenberg or work with a coach. I have adopted some of the concepts of *Nonvio-*

lent Communication and other modalities to create my own methodology with the following five steps.

The first step involves taking a few intentional deep breaths and connecting with your heart before engaging in conversation. This allows you to communicate from the field of love, not from the ego realm. If you have not developed the skill to drop into your heart, you can place your hand on your chest and take a few deep inhales and exhales while repeating silently "I am safe; I can relax." Once you feel you have shifted from an amygdala-based stress response to a calm, non-reactionary state, you can open up to communicate with kindness while respecting your needs. It's also important you use that same kindness and respect when listening to your partner and attempting to understand their needs.

The second step is to listen attentively to discern if the conversation is heading toward moving forward or clearing up the past. Is the conversation revolving around a behavior your partner needs to change? Are you being triggered because there is a part of you that needs to be explored and healed? Notice the important difference in what you are asking—is it something your partner needs to accommodate to suit your needs, or is it something *you* need to transform? The time for asking your partner to change is over; now is the time to take responsibility for how you are going to act, not react, to whatever their actions and words may be.

The third step is to be aware of using the correct, non-confrontational language. Words are the essential tools in building your new relationship, and I advise you to be selective, employing only words that encourage positive behaviors rather than those that reprimand past choices and might create conflict. If heavy emotions come into play, and you or your partner start shifting your language from cooperation to aggression, take a moment to calm down and regroup.

Once you have shifted back to being able to talk and negotiate, ask for permission to have the conversation again. If this is not possible, postpone to a time when everybody has had time to re-center.

The fourth step is to be willing to apologize and admit when you are wrong or have said something inappropriate if anger or resentment seeped into the conversation. This might not happen as you are talking. It takes incredible emotional intelligence to step away from negative feelings to acknowledge our part in them, but you can at least make a point to apologize so resentment is not carried into future conversations.

The fifth step is to give thanks for remaining emotionally neutral and objective so the conversations can be productive instead of destructive. This applies to you and your partner, even if it is not manifesting this way in your current reality. One of my favorite mantras is *"If you believe it, you can live it,"* and I apply it to all situations that do not correlate with my vision. Instead of letting the current reality dictate the outcome, I redouble my visualization efforts to remain focused on the desired resolution. Show gratitude for your partner agreeing to communicate with you and allowing you to be honest and vulnerable. There will be times when you do not reach any agreements, but practicing communication where everyone feels heard and respected is a victory in itself.

STEP 9–
NEGOTIATING FOR WIN-WIN

Learning how to manage your emotions to avoid unconsciously reacting will be the greatest skill you can apply during negotiations. My approach is counterintuitive to our society's messaging to use hatred as a powerful motivator to fight, disregarding the consequences. When we negotiate from a place of animosity, everybody loses because of the emotional costs that are not taken into consideration until it is too late. I teach all my clients a Buddhist practice called tonglen, which I recommend doing before meeting to negotiate with their spouse and legal team. It is the practice of sending love to your enemies or those with whom you are having a disagreement. This causes an energetic shift with the potential to set you up to achieve peaceful and productive negotiations for the divorce settlement.

Start off with a few minutes of deep, slow breaths to calm your mind. Next, send love to someone you truly admire and love. Then, send loving thoughts to yourself, which, depending on how skilled you are at practicing self-love, could be more or less challenging. Either way, do not give up, and visualize yourself happy and filled with love, maybe by bringing forward memories of truly joyful times in your life. Let the feeling of love and contentment wash over you. Finally—and this can be the really hard part, depending on your relationship—send love to your ex and wish them happiness and peace.

After practicing tonglen meditation, check with yourself to see if you are ready to begin negotiations. If so, I suggest following these guidelines:

- Know your rights: Even if you are confident that you and your spouse can negotiate on your own, I strongly advise you consult with a family lawyer to understand your rights and obligations. Every state is different, and each situation is unique, meaning Google and friends' opinions will not suffice. There are services online offering legal coaching and paralegal assistance, and in some cases, they can also provide mediation help. I suggest you explore these options to keep your divorce as affordable and conflict-free as possible.

- Learn to listen without judgment: Listen with the objective of understanding what your ex's needs are. If you feel hurt during a negotiation, instead of responding with harsh words, pause, breathe, and take a step back to return to a place of calm within yourself. Then, ask genuinely non-confrontational questions to understand their request without making any conclusions about their intentions. Remove any preconceived ideas that he or she is trying to "screw you" so you can find the middle ground to continue negotiations.

- Find ways to compromise on a win-win settlement: A successful negotiation is when all parties have most of their demands met. It is best if you can open yourself up to the possibility of *everything* being negotiable, albeit some things more easily than others. Think about all the things your spouse is asking for, and find creative ways to structure deals to fulfill each other's requests. Furthermore, be emotionally prepared for all counteroffers—no matter how ridiculous they seem—without getting offended.

- Trade requests: Some lawyers use strategies to get their client the best possible deal without caring about what the other party receives. I understand this is their responsibility, but it can be a recipe for disaster as the end result tends to be a winner-loser settlement. This kind of arrangement will most likely come back to haunt you later. Whomever was at the losing end might find ways to rebalance the scales, usually translating into high-conflict co-parenting and even appeals and motions to change the settlement. Instead, cooperate with your spouse to reach an agreement where you both get as close to what you want as possible.

- Be willing to respectfully end the negotiation: Unless the negotiation is rooted in respect from both parties, simply refrain from continuing. If you notice that the process is turning into a hateful or resentful exchange, prevent confrontation by asking to postpone the meeting. Take the time to work on the emotions derailing the exchange with the help of a divorce coach or therapist, and kindly ask your partner to reconsider their attitude before you sit down to negotiate again. Request to have another attempt at reaching agreements, and if you do not succeed, suggest involving mediators or lawyers.

- Reach out for help: Not everyone can successfully negotiate with their partner, for a variety of reasons. Do not be discouraged or feel guilty about it—simply reach out for professional help. You might consider using mediation or arbitration, which has a high rate of success. If this step does not work, you can engage lawyers, but be aware that if you cannot reach agreements, the next step might be appearing in front of a judge who will make the final decisions. For those who choose a collaborative divorce, there might be lawyers and mediators involved to assist with a contract, removing the possibility of going through the court system without having to start the process again.

- Always consult a lawyer before signing anything: If, on the other hand, you were successful at negotiating everything with your partner, make sure a reputable family lawyer reviews the documents for any legal pitfalls before you agree to the terms. Your rights will be protected, and you will minimize the risk of potential appeals and costly litigation later on.

STEP 10—
CELEBRATE

Although there is a large spectrum of how painful and complicated divorce can get, there is one constant: it always ends. When things get difficult and you want to give up, focus on how closing this chapter will open up an endless field of possibilities for your future. Before you step into that next great chapter, take some time to celebrate how powerful and strong you truly are. Divorce most likely taught you that you can overcome even the most difficult obstacles to become the best version of yourself.

This is no small feat, and I hope you can join me in my deepest admiration for what you just achieved. Create the time and space to celebrate *you* so you can have a memory of this momentous occasion. Use your imagination and resources to whatever degree you feel comfortable—it can be as little as treating yourself to your favorite spa, going out for dinner with friends, or signing up for a retreat or trip. Whatever you choose, make sure you commit to doing it as soon as your divorce is over. I gave myself a trip to Costa Rica for a seven-day retreat to work with plant medicine. That trip began my love affair with this magical land where, five years later, I am building a house with my beloved husband. I see you, and I celebrate you!

CHAPTER 5

POST-DIVORCE

In this chapter, I will give you a quick overview of the areas I see most of my clients fret about most after the papers are signed so you can avoid sweating the small stuff. I'll also offer you a taste of all the beauty that exists once you reach the end of the divorce tunnel. Here is the undiluted truth about post-divorce life to help you navigate it with grace and compassion for yourself and your ex.

Co-Parenting And Parallel Parenting

Let's start with some of the main questions that cause us to lose sleep over getting a divorce: How is the relationship with my children go-

ing to change? How will I co-parent with someone I might disagree
with? How will I handle being a single mom/dad?

First, I want to make an important semantic distinction with
deep ramifications in your mindset. In my opinion, a single parent is someone who is raising children entirely on their own with
no support financially or emotionally from the other parent. The
father or mother has completely removed themselves (by choice
or not) from any parental responsibilities, and it all falls on you.
Based on this assumption, being a divorced parent sharing custody
does not qualify as being a single parent because you are receiving
support to one degree or another. Unless you assume full custody
and have no child support (and it's rare any court will approve that
kind of settlement), you are not a single parent—you are a divorced
parent. My preference in the majority of cases is that parents aim
for as close to 50/50 custody as possible. Obviously, there might
be reasons why this is not feasible, and each situation should be
reviewed individually before making any decisions. Your relationship with your children will indeed change, but in my experience
and in that of many of my clients, it actually gets better. Spending
time away from our children gives us the chance to delve into our
passions, careers, and relationships, allowing time with the kids to
be a fully present experience.

Co-parenting might evolve into parallel parenting when disagreements abound with the other parent. You can learn over time
to respect how different parenting approaches do not mean there is
a right and wrong way of raising children. It is not necessary for a
child to have two identical households—they can learn pretty quickly that there are differing rules or behaviors to follow at each home.
As long as their safety is not compromised, you might have to put
your ego aside and not launch into conflict because your ex wants to

follow a different protocol when it comes to eating, relaxing, screen time, or even language. If kids can learn how to coexist in different environments, we adults can surely learn to respect them too.

Financial Independence

The second biggest post-divorce struggle after parenting issues is financial instability. I have seen it all: everything from clients going from financial wreckage during their marriage to becoming savvy financial wizards, to others taking the opposite journey from riches to rags. I am now convinced your financial success depends equally on how well you managed the financial settlement and your mindset toward money. I could write an entire book on ways to improve your finances, but honestly, there are already plenty out there. The few suggestions I would offer are:

- Create a financial settlement that is not aimed at keeping one of the parties dependent on the other: you do not want your financial future tied to someone else with whom you might not want to interact.

- Educate yourself about finances: Even if during your marriage you were not involved, you can learn everything you need to know through books, courses, and mentors. Do not be afraid to seem ignorant at first. Everybody starts with little or no knowledge, and it is up to you to become financially literate.

- Identify different sources of income: The wealthiest people in the world do not rely on one job or single source of income; they have several active and passive money-generating activities. Some of my clients went from "stay-at-home moms" with no income to running six-figure businesses in the online and affiliate world. We all have gifts and talents we can monetize. It is just a matter of being courageous and making it happen.

- Do whatever is necessary to reprogram your mind from limiting, scarcity-ridden beliefs to empowering abundant ones: Most of this conditioning comes from our childhood, and although we are not responsible for acquiring the beliefs, we are responsible for removing them. Mindset, followed by skillset, are the strong foundations for wealth. Do not let your financial past obscure your future success.

Dating

Depending on the type of relationship expert you listen to, you will find contradictory advice everywhere: Start dating only after one year has passed. Get back on the horse right away. Heal for as long as needed, then think about dating. Online is the way to go! In-person dating creates real connections. And so on, and on, and on. No wonder so many people are reluctant and intimidated at the prospect of dating! Giving dating advice is certainly not my specialty, but there is so much apprehension around the prospect of dating post-divorce that I am taking the liberty of making a couple suggestions.

First and foremost, listen to your intuition. You truly know better than anyone else what you need and when you need it. However, before you give your energy to anyone else, you might need to get to know yourself better first. Cherish the empty space to honor, grieve, and integrate the learnings from your past relationship before diving into a new commitment. Some people are wired to do that alone; others prefer to do so while in a relationship. I am a firm believer that you can focus on yourself and clearly hear the messages your soul is trying to tell you *and* be in a partnership. They are not exclusionary realms, but it is up to you to decide if you need alone time to regroup or if you prefer healing in company. I also encourage my clients to view dating as an easy and fun endeavor. Approach the whole process as a way to meet new people, with finding your Prince or Princess Charming as a potential added bonus. It's best to detach from the outcome and simply enjoy the process. With the rising number of couples divorcing and online options to meet people, gone are the days when you were out of luck finding a new partner after divorce. We are no longer limited by our geography, work, or friends as the only variables determining if we will find our soulmate.

With the inception of social media, we now show our life in an electronic format to both the people we know and those we have never met. This has created a repeated distortion of real life versus filtered, curated, and edited social life and has produced interesting changes in the way we start and maintain relationships. I polled my social media following about relationships, and the result was a variety of views about the influence of social media on creating beliefs for what is possible in dating and relationships. Some people described love and relationships with the following statements:

- Dating begins on an app interaction and is reduced to an exchange of texts and pics.

- Feelings of connection or interest are to be subdued and not shared.

- Sex is easier to find than a plumber for a Friday night emergency.

- Conversations have been replaced with "Netflix and chill."

- Love is synonymous with co-dependence.

- Insecurities don't get resolved in the context of intimacy but are surgically removed.

- Exclusivity is only given to your phone provider.

- "Commitment" is the kind of word that sends people running for the hills.

At the other end of the spectrum, there was a more hopeful message:

- Some apps have made the dating process more selective and efficient while simultaneously opening up the dating pool.

- More than ever, men and women are healing their past by doing Inner Work facilitated by the knowledge shared on social media.

- Society is becoming more accepting of new containers for relationships and allowing individuals to be in charge of how they want their unions to be.

- Financial freedom provides full autonomy to choose being in a partnership or single.

I believe all options are acceptable, and it is entirely up to each individual to choose what they want for their romantic future. Just be aware that #relationshipgoals might not be a genuine standard for what is possible, and you should not be ashamed if your post-divorce dating life is far from rainbows and unicorns. Enjoy the process, and at the right time, the right person for your soul evolution will show up.

Remarrying

A new theory I am testing revolves around the idea that maybe we got the concept of marriage wrong. We usually get married as young, immature individuals with little experience or wisdom around relationships and almost nonexistent knowledge about who we truly are or what we need and want. We tend to have overly romanticized ideas about how our relationship will evolve, and we are rarely taught how to communicate consciously and resolve arguments without leaving residual pain and resentment. We are also poorly skilled at understanding the cycles relationships go through, and we are unprepared for the peaks and valleys. Some people make every possible mistake within the first marriage but use divorce as a catalyst to learn emotional and relational skills and are now thriving in the second marriage or subsequent relationships.

Maybe we are not supposed to live happily ever after with our first spouse. Maybe we do not know how to truly love or be loved in the first marriage, and the stressors of trying to get ahead in life while raising children are insurmountable. Maybe we can look at our first marriage not as the final destination but as our initial lesson in the school of relationships. Maybe we should normalize that first marriages are not meant to last forever but to teach us about ourselves and help us develop a degree of emotional maturity and more realistic expectations for our future partners.

When you ask divorcees if they are willing to remarry, there is no unanimous answer. Due to the pervasive belief that divorce equates to failure, many are jaded after their first marriages, and some may struggle to compromise their newfound freedom in another monogamous, lifelong marriage. The question of whether to marry again or not is such a personal one, but in my opinion, getting clear on how you will show up in your next relationship is far more important than any marriage certificate. For me, the fundamentals for any new relationship are:

- You are prepared to give them your best and gently push them to be their best.

- You both recognize that open and honest communication is nonnegotiable, and you are both accountable for keeping it that way.

- Each partner does the Inner Work necessary to heal past traumas and wounds so they do not self-sabotage the new partnership.

You might find a partner for the rest of your life or for a season. Love and honor your partner while you have them. Be prepared to let them go if your relationship has been completed and you have learned all the lessons you were meant to teach each other.

Healing

This book promised to deliver a practical ten-step process for healing, and now that you've made it this far, you might be asking, "Where is my 'I Am Healed' badge?" The truth is that no number of books, workshops, or teachers can give you the healing you crave and rightly deserve. Learning and healing cannot happen at this level of rational consciousness—they have to be felt and embodied. I hope this book helps to show you the way, to plant the seeds, and to inspire you, through my own example and my clients' transformations, to take the first step in the journey toward your healing. Once you say yes to that, the rest will unfold in its own divine timing. All that is required is that you keep applying the skills and methodologies I shared for every aspect of your healing.

It is my belief that we do not come here to teach; we come here to love and be loved. Pure and genuine love is the ultimate teacher. No other human, religion, or entity can provide you with that. Healing is the return to our hearts and that infinite capacity for love we had when we were born but lost in the process of adulting. If you are committing to your healing, you are saying yes to love—a magnificent, all-encompassing, all-forgiving kind of love—and that is not an easy feat in this world. Whenever you are hurting and wish for the pain to go away, ask yourself: Where am I not loving enough? Where is love trying to be expressed through me? What people in my life (myself included) need more love? Go ahead and generate that love. It is inside of you; you just have to learn where to locate it so you can access the endless reservoir of kindness and compassion available to all of us.

We learn about love as little kids from our family, caregivers, teachers, and friends, and most of our healing revolves around resolving unprocessed traumas from that period of our lives. From the moment we are conceived up to age seven, we are creating the set of beliefs that will dictate what our adult life will look like. We subconsciously learn to create our future reality by observing and making assumptions about our environments. It is like programming a computer with the software needed to function. Depending on the environment in which we grew up, we might have developed the emotional intelligence to deal with our emotions because we were allowed to express and integrate them as children. We might be courageous if speaking our truth was safe. We might have trust issues and difficulty with intimacy if someone we loved left and we had no support to process the loss. As adults, we carry our original conditioning, including fears and disempowering beliefs, from the past into our present-day relationships. You are not responsible for the damaging beliefs that were passed on to you, but you owe it to yourself and your children to transmute that pain into a purpose that creates a better world.

Just as importantly, as we embark on the journey of healing ourselves, we are also healing the suffering of the generations before and after us. Once we break the stigma and embrace the new paradigm that divorce is empowering instead of traumatizing, we will disrupt the cycle of shame for the coming generations, starting with our own children. Despite how challenging divorce can be, it has the potential to be a blessing in disguise and the rite of passage to initiate you in the healing modalities that are most appropriate for you. My divorce was the place of despair where I was broken down enough to allow the breakthroughs to unfold and show me who I truly am and what my mission is. I cannot imagine living life without the self-awareness that the ending of my first marriage gifted me, plus all the knowledge and skills it helped me develop. I hope you can also use this transformation to realign with the magnificent soul you are and allow your light to shine bright. The world truly needs fulfilled, happy, and healed individuals who are not enslaved by an outdated contract they have outgrown. Remember, if you can believe it, you can live it.

CONCLUSION

It is my utmost desire that this book is your trusted companion, keeping you safe as you navigate the challenging oceans of divorce. I have committed my life's purpose to ensure that nobody is left behind in this process. Please reach out if you need more help and personalized guidance. I want every single one of you to have the chance to share your story, all the lessons you are learning, and the healing modalities that are assisting you. I beg everyone reading these pages to be courageous, stand up, and share your voice so we can fulfill our emotional needs of being heard, seen, and loved. This is how we heal our collective selves.

My cry for a peaceful uprising to dismantle the old-school paradigm asks that you take a minute or two to write down, audio record, or videotape your story and email it to me at info@divorceforlove.com. If you are brave enough, post it on your social media with #divorcedtoo, and let the world know that you are growing through (or grew through) divorce, despite how painful it might be. Show others you are a peace warrior, and choose to usher in a new earth consciousness by having a Holistic Divorce. We need to sit in a circle again, tell our stories, and share our truth so we can learn and walk each other home.

I am no teacher or healer; I am simply someone learning and healing and would love to leave you with a parting gift in the form of seeds for your consciousness: the eternal truths I am uncovering during my healing journey. Use your intuition to take what resonates and leave what does not. I love every single one of you for waking up to a higher reality of love and unity, and it is my ultimate hope that your divorce helps you get there. Aloha and Mahalo ke Akua.

To generate and maintain conscious love, we must be willing to bring our conditioned belief structure to the light to be examined and released as needed. Create space for yourself and the new version that wants to come to life. Allow yourself to receive. Know that you are worth whatever your soul is asking for. Feel deeply. All the feels. Process and let go through the power of forgiveness. Holding onto past pain and grievances stops the healing process. Grow outside of your comfort zone every day. Laugh at fear. Cry all the rivers of your heart. Welcome change. Embrace endings instead of resisting them. Become a lover of all things, situations, creatures, and humans. Let love be your teacher. Stop searching for love, and become LOVE.